• Bartholomew

WALK THE PEAK
by Brian Spencer

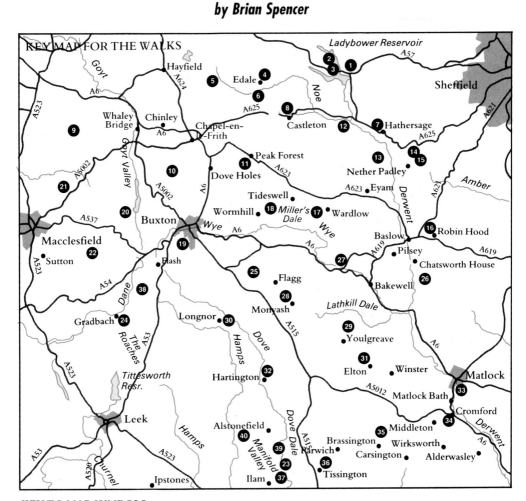

KEY MAP FOR THE WALKS

Ladybower Reservoir
A57
Sheffield

Govt
Hayfield
A624
A6
Edale 4
5
6
A625
8
Noe
A625

A523
Whaley Bridge
Chinley
Chapel-en--Frith
A6
Castleton
12
7 Hathersage
A625
14
15

9
A5002
Peak Forest
11
Dove Holes
A623
13
Nether Padley

21
Goyt Valley
10
A5002
Tideswell
Wormhill
18 Miller's Dale 17 Wardlow
A623 Eyam
Derwent
Amber

20
Buxton
Wye A6
Wye
Baslow
A619 Pilsey
16 Robin Hood
A619

Macclesfield
22
Sutton
19
Flash
25
Flagg
27
Chatsworth House
Bakewell
26

A54
Dane
38
28
Monyash
Lathkill Dale

Gradbach 24
The Roaches
A53
Longnor 30
Hamps
Dove
A515
29 Youlgreave
A6

Tittesworth Resr.
Hartington
32
31
Elton Winster
Matlock
33
A5012 Matlock Bath

Leek
Hamps
A523
Alstonefield
40
Manifold Valley
39
Parwich
Brassington 35 Middleton
Wirksworth
Cromford
34
Derwent
A6

A53
A520
Churnet
Ipstones
Ilam
23
37
36 Tissington
Carsington Alderwasley

KEY TO MAP SYMBOLS

Main Road	Railway	Cairn	Information Centre
Minor Road	Description of viewpoint	Slope or Crags	Youth Hostel
Track and Footpath	Viewpoint	Woods	Church or Abbey
Route of Walk	Summit	Parking	Site of Antiquity

Published by Bartholomew
HarperCollins*Publishers*,
77-85 Fulham Palace Road
LONDON W6 8JB

A catalogue record for this book is available from the British
Library.

First published 1987
Revised editions published 1988, 1990
This revised edition published 1993

ISBN 0 7028 2201 9   MNM 87/4/45

1 WALKING IN THE PEAK DISTRICT

When walking in the Peak you can encounter four quite different types of terrain. Probably the easiest walking of all is on the limestone plateau where stone stiles and green lanes indicate the way. In the dales, paths wander through shady woodland and follow bubbling trout rivers. In the north, the unpredictable weather makes navigation across the trackless moors quite difficult. Gritstone edges above the Derwent, or the lower heather moors, are more straightforward and the footpaths are easier to follow.

Walking is a sport which can fulfil the needs of everyone. You can adapt it to suit your own preferences and it is the healthiest of activities. Your inclination might be to walk two or three miles along a gentle track instead of one of the more arduous long distance routes but, whatever the walk, it will always improve your general well-being. Walking should be anything from an individual pastime to a family stroll, or maybe a group of friends enjoying the fresh air and open spaces of our countryside. There is no need for walking to be competitive and, to get the most from walking, it shouldn't be regarded simply as a means of covering a given distance in the shortest possible time.

As with all other outdoor activities, walking is safe provided a few simple common sense rules are followed:−

a Make sure you are fit enough to complete the walk.

b Always try to let others know where you intend going.

c Be clothed adequately for the weather and always wear suitable footwear.

d Always allow plenty of time for the walk, especially if it is longer or harder than you have done before.

e Whatever the distance you plan to walk, always allow plenty of daylight hours unless you are absolutely certain of the route.

f If mist or bad weather come on unexpectedly do not panic and try to remember the last certain feature which you have passed (road, farm, wood, etc.). Then work out your route from that point on the map but be sure of your route before continuing.

g Do not dislodge stones on the high edges: there may be climbers or other walkers on the lower crags and slopes.

h Unfortunately, accidents can happen even on the easiest of walks. If this should be the case and you need the help of others, make sure that the injured person is safe in a place where no further injury is likely to occur. For example, the injured person should not be left on a steep hillside or in danger from falling rocks. If you cannot leave anyone with the injured person and, even if they are conscious, try to leave a written note explaining their injuries and whatever you have done in the way of first aid treatment. Make sure you know exactly where you left them and then go to find assistance. If you meet a National Park Ranger, tell him or her what has happened. Otherwise, make your way to a telephone and dial 999 and ask for assistance. Unless the accident has happened within easy access of a road, then it is the responsibility of the Police to arrange evacuation. Always give accurate directions of how to find the casualty and, if possible, give an indication of the injuries involved.

i When walking in open country, learn to keep an eye on the immediate foreground while you admire the scenery or plan the route ahead. This may sound difficult, especially to a beginner but, once you can adapt to this method, your enjoyment will increase.

j It's best to walk at a steady pace, always on the flat of the feet as this is less tiring. Try not to walk directly up or downhill. A zig-zag route is a more comfortable way of negotiating a slope. Running directly downhill is a major cause of erosion on popular hillsides.

k When walking along a country road, walk on the right, facing the traffic. The exception to this rule is, when approaching a blind bend, the walker should cross over to the left and so have a clear view and also be seen in both directions.

l Finally, always park your car where it will not cause inconvenience to other road users or prevent a farmer from gaining access to his fields. Make sure that you lock your car and hide any valuables before leaving or, perferably, carry all valuables with you.

2 EQUIPMENT

Equipment, including clothing, footwear and rucksacks, is essentially a personal thing and depends on several factors, such as the type of activity planned, the time of year and weather likely to be encountered.

All too often, a novice walker will spend pounds on a fashionable jacket but will skimp when it comes to buying footwear or a comfortable rucksack. Blistered and tired feet quickly remove all enjoyment from even the most exciting walk and a poorly balanced rucksack will soon feel as though it is carrying half a hundredweight. Well designed equipment is not only more comfortable but, being better made, it is longer lasting.

Clothing should be adequate for the day. In summer, remember to protect your head and neck which are particularly vulnerable in a strong sun. Wear light woollen socks and lightweight boots or strong shoes will be adequate. A spare pullover and waterproofs carried in the rucksack should, however, always be there in case you need them.

Winter wear is a much more serious affair. Remember that once the body starts to lose heat it becomes much less efficient. Jeans are particularly unsuitable for winter wear and can sometimes even be downright dangerous.

Waterproof clothing is an area where it pays to buy the best you can afford. Make sure that the jacket is loose-fitting, has a generous hood and comes down at least to knee level. Waterproof overtrousers will not only offer complete protection in the rain but they are also windproof. Do not be misled by flimsy nylon 'showerproof' affairs. Remember, too, that garments made from rubberised or plastic material are heavy to carry and wear and they trap body condensation. Your rucksack should have wide, padded carrying straps for comfort.

It is important to wear boots that fit well or shoes with a good moulded sole – blisters can ruin any walk! Woollen socks are much more comfortable than any other fibre. Your clothes should be comfortable and not likely to catch on twigs and bushes. In winter, it's best to take two lightweight jumpers, one at least with a crew neck. You will find this better than wearing one jumper made of heavy material. Your jacket should have a hood and it should be windproof and loose enough for an extra layer of warmer clothing underneath. A woollen hat, which can be pulled well down, is essential in winter.

A piece of semi-rigid plastic foam carried in the rucksack makes a handy and yet almost weightless seat for open-air picnics.

An area map, as well as this guide, is useful for accurate navigation and it adds to the enjoyment of a walk. Finally, a small first aid kit is an invaluable help in coping with cuts and other small injuries.

3 PUBLIC RIGHTS OF WAY

Although most of the area covered by this guide comes within the authority of the Peak National Park, this does not mean that there is complete freedom of access to walk anywhere. Much of the land within the park is privately owned and what might appear to be an ideal spot for a picnic, or somewhere to exercise the dog, is often part of another person's livelihood.

In 1949 the National Parks and Access to the Countryside Act tidied up the law covering rights of way. Following public consultation, maps were drawn up by the Countryside Authorities of England and Wales to show all the rights of way. Copies of these maps are available for public inspection and are invaluable when trying to resolve doubts over little used footpaths. Once on the map, the right of way is irrefutable.

Right of way means that anyone may walk freely on a defined footpath or ride a horse or pedal cycle along a public bridleway. No-one may interfere with this right and the walker is within his rights if he removes any obstruction along the route, provided that he has not set out purposely with the intention of removing that obstruction. All obstructions should be reported to the local Highways Authority.

Free access to footpaths and bridleways does mean that certain guidelines should be followed as courtesy to those who live and work in the area. For example, you should only sit down to picnic where it does not interfere with other walkers or the landowner. All gates must be closed to prevent stock from straying and dogs must be kept under close control — usually this is interpreted as meaning that they should be kept on a leash. Motor vehicles must not be driven along a public footpath or bridleway without the landowner's consent.

A farmer can put a docile mature beef bull with a herd of cows or heifers, in a field crossed by a public footpath. Beef bulls such as Herefords (usually brown/red colour) are unlikely to be upset by passers-by but dairy bulls, like the black and white Friesian, can be dangerous by nature. It is, therefore, illegal for a farmer to let a dairy bull roam loose in a field open to public access.

Most public rights of way within the Peak National Park have been clearly defined and are marked as such on available maps. They are marked on the Ordnance Survey one inch (1:63360) and metric (1:50000) maps as red dots for footpaths and red dashes for bridleways. On the OS 1:25000 scale, the dots and dashes are green. (Red dots and dashes on the 1:25000 Outdoor Leisure Maps indicate permitted footpaths and bridleways respectively). All of the walks in this guide cover routes which follow the public right of way.

4 THE COUNTRY CODE

The Country Code has been designed not as a set of hard and fast rules, although they do have the backing of the law, but as a statement of common-sense. The code is a gentle reminder of how to behave in the countryside. Walkers should walk with the intention of leaving the place exactly as it was before they arrived. There is an old saying that a good walker 'leaves only footprints and takes only photographs', which really sums up the code perfectly.

Never walk more than two abreast on a footpath as you will erode more ground causing an unnatural widening of paths. Also try to avoid the spread of trodden ground around a boggy area. Mud soon cleans off boots but plant life is slow to grow back once it has been worn away.

Have respect for everything in the countryside, be it those beautiful flowers found along the way or a farmer's gate which is difficult to close.

Stone walls were built at a time when labour costs were a fraction of those today and the special skills required to build or repair them have almost disappeared. Never climb over or on to stone walls: always use stiles and gates.

Dogs which chase sheep can cause them to lose their lambs and a farmer is within his rights if he shoots a dog which he believes is worrying his stock.

The moors and woodlands are often tinder dry in summer, so take care not to start a fire. A fire caused by something as simple as a discarded cigarette can burn for weeks, once it gets deep down into the underlying peat.

When walking across fields or enclosed land, make sure that you read the map carefully and avoid trespassing. As a rule, the line of a footpath or right of way, even when it is not clearly defined on the ground, can usually be followed by lining up stiles or gates.

5 MAP READING

Some people find map reading so easy that they can open a map and immediately relate it to the area of countryside in which they are standing. To others a map is as unintelligible as ancient Greek! A map is an accurate but flat picture of the three dimensional features of the countryside. Features such as roads, streams, woodlands and buildings are relatively easy to identify, either from their shape or position. Heights, on the other hand, can be difficult to interpret from the single dimension of a map. The one inch (1:63360) maps indicate every 50 foot contour line, while the metricated 1:25000 and 1:50000 maps give the contours at 10 metre intervals. Summits and spot heights are also shown.

The best way to estimate the angle of a slope, as shown on any map, is to remember that if the contour lines come close together then the slope is steep — the closer the steeper.

Learn the symbols for features shown on the map and, when starting out on a walk, line up the map with one or more feature, which is recognisable both from the map and on the ground. In this way the map will be correctly positioned relative to the terrain. It should only be necessary to look from the map towards the footpath or objective of your walk and then make for it! This process is also useful for determining your position at any time during the walk.

Let's take the skill of map reading one stage further: sometimes there are no easily recognisable features nearby: there may be the odd clump of trees and a building or two but none of them can be exactly related to the map. This is a frequent occurence but there is a simple answer to the problem and this is where the use of a compass comes in. Simply place the map on the ground, or other flat surface, with the compass held gently above the map. Turn the map until the edge is parallel to the line of the compass needle, which should point to the top of the map. Lay the compass on the map and adjust the position of both, making sure that the compass needle still points to the top of the map and is parallel to the edge. By this method, the map is orientated in a north-south alignment. To find your position on the map, look out for prominent features and draw imaginary lines from them down on to the map. Your position is where these lines cross. This method of map reading takes a little practice before you can become proficient but it is worth the effort.

It is all too easy for members of a walking group to leave map reading to the skilled member or members of the party. No one is perfect and even the best map reader can make mistakes. Other members of the group should take the trouble to follow the route on the map, so that any errors are spotted before they cause problems.

Once you become proficient at map reading, you will learn to estimate the length of time required for a walk. Generally, you should estimate an extra 5 minutes for every 100 ft (30.5m) you walk uphill.

6 THE PEAK DISTRICT NATIONAL PARK

In many other countries, National Parks are wilderness areas, where few people live unless they are connected with running the park. Countries such as the United States of America have even gone to the length of moving residents off land designated as a National Park. In England and Wales, National Parks are areas of outstanding beauty where people still live and work. One of the major functions of a National Park is to preserve the landscape and the livelihoods of the people living within its boundaries. This is achieved by careful planning control. The National Parks and Access to the Countryside Act of 1949 led to the formation of the nine National Parks in England and Wales. The Peak National Park was designated as such in 1951.

The word 'National' in the title sometimes leads to misunderstanding. National Parks are not nationalised or in any way owned by the government. Most of the land within the park is privately owned by the people who live and work there — be they farmers, private landowners or quarry owners. Certain areas of scenic beauty and ancient buildings around the Peak District are owned by The National Trust but these were left as gifts by far-sighted owners as a means of ensuring their preservation.

The Peak National Park extends over 542 square miles (1404 sq.km). Divided into two uniquely different zones, with wild gritstone moors to the north and gentler limestone uplands and dales to the south, it is surrounded by millions of people living in the industrial areas of England. With the advent of motorways the Peak is accessible to the bulk of the population in under two hours. The Peak District was the first National Park and is the most visited.

Administration of the park is controlled by a committee composed, on a proportional basis of representatives of the surrounding County and Metropolitan Councils and two District Councils as well as members appointed by the Secretary of State for the Environment.

One of the statutory functions of a Park Authority is the appointment of full-time and voluntary Park Rangers. These are people with particular knowledge of some aspects of the local environment who are available to give help and advice to visitors. Other functions of the Ranger Service include giving assistance to local farmers in such matters as rebuilding damaged walls to prevent stock from straying and leading guided walks from one of the Information Centres. Permanent Information Centres are based at Edale, Castleton and Bakewell.

Probably the most important responsibility of the Peak National Park, from the point of view of the walker, is the negotiation of access agreements across open moorland. During the late 1920s and early 1930s, rambling grew in popularity as workers from the industrial towns looked for a means of escaping their crowded existence. The obvious place for this escape was to the high moors which were jealously guarded by their owners, who used them for grouse shooting. Pressures caused by the demand for easy and free access often led to conflicts of interest.

Several ramblers, mainly the alleged ring leaders, were arrested and received sentences ranging from two to six months but they had made their point. One of the first tasks the Peak National Park set itself after its formation in 1951 was to negotiate access agreements. These were not always straightforward but, by careful and diplomatic negotiation, agreements have been reached with farmers and landowners giving free access to most of the high moors of the Dark Peak. In all, a total of 76 square miles (197km^2) of moorland, including Kinder Scout, are open to unrestricted walking and rock climbing apart from a few days in summer when sections of the moors are closed for grouse shooting. Notices are published locally showing the dates when the moors are closed and there are also signposts giving dates at access points to the moors.

Losehill Hall National Park Study Centre is a converted Victorian mansion which is set in spaciously wooded grounds to the south of Lose Hill. Residential and day courses are held on a wide variety of topics ranging from environmental studies, archaeology and the National Park and the pressures it faces, to hill walking, cycling, caving and more specialised subjects.

7 WHAT IS THE PEAK DISTRICT?

The title 'Peak District' is something of a misnomer. For a start there are only two or three hills in the district which can claim to represent the true conical shape of a peak. The name 'Peak', in fact, refers to a tribe who lived in the area in ancient times. In the year 924, a cleric writing about the hills and dales of what is now North Derbyshire, referred to the inhabitants as living in 'Peaclond' and the name seems to have stuck. 'Peac' comes from the old English for knoll or hill: there is a hilly or mountainous meaning to the title, but certainly not peaks in the strictest sense. Another Old English reference occurs in the use of 'low' which comes from 'hlaw' meaning a mound or a hill. No wonder visitors are often confused — peaks where there are none and high points called lows!

There are really two Peak Districts — Dark and White. Two areas so completely different that, when standing on the breezy limestone plateau of the White Peak, it is hard to imagine that the untamed wilderness of Bleaklow and Kinder Scout are not far away.

Broadly speaking, the Peak District can be sub-divided into six distinct areas.

a. The most northerly is the wildest and covers the moors above Saddleworth and the Longdendale Valley with the huge spread of Bleaklow filling the space between Longdendale and the Snake Pass.

b. Kinder Scout is a vast boggy plateau bordered to its south by Edale and the graceful sweep of the Mam Tor/Rushup Edge Ridge.

c. To the east, rising above the Derwent Valley, there is a long escarpment which is clearly defined by a series of gritstone edges backed by heather moorland.

d. In the west, gritstone crags range from The Roaches above Leek to Windgather Rocks and Castle Naze on the northern limits. High open moors offer miles of lesser known walking. Tranquil wooded valleys cutting the western moors are excellent places to walk on hot summer days.

e. Limestone makes its most northerly appearance in dramatic cliffs and knolls above Castleton, a place of caves and ancient lead mines. South of Castleton are some of the highest villages in the White Peak. They can expect to be cut off by deep snow for several days during most winters.

f. The limestone plateau to the southwest of the A6 is incised by deep valleys and is judged by many to be the prettiest part of the Peak. It is certainly a zone of contrasts where the lush pastures of the rolling uplands have been grazed by cattle since time immemorial. Rivers run pure and clear and they are full of lively trout.

People came early to the Peak. Settling first on the treeless limestone plateau, they left mysterious mounds and stone cirles. The circle at Arbor Low between Hartington and Youlgreave was probably the most important. Certainly its surrounding earthworks indicate its significance. Arbor Low is unique as the stones lie flat, unlike the more normal uprights associated with other circles. Early man hunted in the Dark Peak, following the seasonal migrations of game across moorland then covered by scrubby birch and mountain ash. Oak trees filled most of the valleys and dales and made them impregnable until later dwellers cut the trees down for fuel and building material. During later and less settled eras, massive earthworks were constructed at different times on top of Mam Tor and at Carl Wark.

Lead brought the Romans into the Peak. The metal, which was mined long before their arrival, attracted them to the area and they established their main centre at *Lutadarum*. Lead ingots embossed with this name have been found and an archaeological survey indicates that *Lutadarum* was probably near Wirksworth. Further north, a fort was built at *Navio* below the village of Hope, to control the hostile natives.

Following the Norman Conquest, the northern part of the Peak was designated a royal game forest or *frith* (hence Chapel-en-le-Frith).

William Peveril, illegitimate son of the Conquerer, had a castle built on an easily defendable crag above Castleton. The castle controlled the King's lead mining interests as well as providing a base for hunting expeditions.

During the Middle Ages, most of the lands were owned by various monasteries. They continued to exploit the resources of lead, which was then very much in demand both as a roofing material and for constructing pipes to supply water into a growing number of monastic establishments. The monks opened large tracts of arable grazing and produced wool to clothe an expanding population. Farms which today have the word Grange as part of their name, were owned by rich monastries until their dissolution by Henry VIII.

Great houses have been built in the Peak. Some are well known, like Chatsworth with its parkland, which was landscaped by Capability Brown, or Haddon Hall — a uniquely preserved medieval country house. There are also many lesser-known stately homes throughout the district which are just as interesting. Most are in private hands, like Tissington Hall which has been owned by the same family for generations. Hartington Hall, a fine example of a Jacobean yeoman's house is now a youth hostel as is Ilam Hall which is an early Victorian mansion preserved by the National Trust.

Customs and festivals abound in the Peak: a unique and charming custom is 'well dressing'. Pictures, usually of a bibical theme, are made from colourful petals, mosses and twigs stuck onto wet clay. The origins of this delightful custom, which offers thanks for the plentiful supply of water on the dry limestone plateau, are lost in the mists of time. A dozen or so villages dress their wells each year and details of the dates are included in the Peak Park's calendar of events. Local Shrovetide customs include the pancake race in Winster and a football match in Ashbourne where almost anything goes. A more tranquil custom is the Castleton Garland Procession. Although linked to ancient fertility rites, it always takes place on 29 May (Oak Apple Day) in commemoration of the restoration to the throne of Charles II. Also, the annual 'Love Feast' is held on the first Sunday in July in a barn in Alport Dale, high above Snake Road. This is a link with times when dissenting worshippers, who disagreed with the 'Act of Uniformity' tying them to the Church of England, had to find seclusion away from the attentions of the troops of the reinstated King Charles II. Forest Chapel, near Wildboarclough, has a rush bearing ceremony on the Sunday nearest to 12 August each year.

Visitors to the Peak can buy jewellery made from Blue John, a semi precious stone found only beneath Treak Cliff, near Castleton. Another Peak novelty is the Bakewell Pudding (never call it a tart!). This delicacy was first made accidently by a 19th-century cook working in the Rutland Arms Hotel. Very fine Stilton cheese is made at the dairy in Hartington from the milk of Peakland cows.

Famous writers have penned the virtues of the Peak but none has better links than Izaak Walton, who fished *The Dove* with Charles Cotton.

Industry has always made it mark. Pack horse, or

'jaggers' tracks can still be followed on foot over the northern moors. Saltways crossed the southern dales. Water-powered mills in the early part of the Industrial Revolution brought textile production to the dales. Florspar, a nuisance to the early lead miners, is now extracted by open cast mining and used as a flux in steel making and as the basis for a number of chemicals.

Today, without any doubt, it is quarrying which makes the greatest industrial impact on the face of the Peak District. Limestone, suitable either as road aggregates or for cement making, is only found in scenically attractive areas and, as a result, the quarries can make an ugly scar on the landscape unless they are carefully monitored.

8 GEOLOGY

The rocks which made the foundations of the Peak District were laid down millions of years ago in a warm sea. Miriads of sea creatures living on the slimy bottom built up the great depth of limestone. Tropical lagoons were fringed by coral reefs which, through time, have become the rounded hills of Thorpe Cloud, Parkhouse and Chrome Hills in Dove Dale. Minor volcanic activity took place during this time. The best examples of this can be found in the small outcrops of basalt near Castleton and in the dolerite quarry which is part of the Tideswell Dale Nature Trail. Lead found its way in gaseous form, through minute cracks in the underlying rocks, laying down the basis of what became a major industry thousands of centuries later. Copper was also deposited in this way, occurring beneath Ecton Hill in the Manifold valley.

A mighty river delta flooded into the tropical sea, depositing mud and sand which consolidated to make the gritstones of the Dark Peak and the shales of Mam Tor.

Gradually, the layers of limestone and gritstone bulged from pressures deep within the earth and the middle and edges split. Ice action later honed the land into the beginning of the Peak District's rocky pattern. At the end of the Ice Age, huge volumes of melt water continued this shaping. The water carved caverns within the limestone of Castleton and Matlock as well as the pot holes of Eldon and it also created the beautiful dales. The land tilted as it buckled to give west facing gritstone outcrops on both sides of the Peak.

9 WILDLIFE IN THE PEAK

Grouse spend their hardy lives on the high moors of the Dark Peak feeding on the tender shoots of young heather. Their tough existence is rudely shattered for four months of every year beginning on the 'Glorious Twelfth of August'. Not so common, and regrettably often shot by mistake, are their cousins the black grouse. Birds of prey have their chosen areas and many migrants, some quite rare, visit quieter sanctuaries on the moors from time to time. Mountain hares are common despite an inability to quickly shed their winter camouflage once the snows have gone. Foxes live a frugal life, mainly dependent upon voles and other small creatures. Plant life on the acid moors has to be tough to combat the extreme weather conditions. Heathers, coarse grass and berry plants such as bilberry, cloudberry and crowberry manage to survive in this harsh environment.

The limestone plateau is much more gentle. It is mainly given over to grazing and masses of colourful flowers still fill the hayfields and road verges. Scabious, meadow cranesbill and other plants, which were once scarce, have made a recent comeback in fields where far-sighted farmers have moved back to natural and cheaper methods of fertilising the land. Plant, and to a certain extent animal life, in the dales depend on the underlying strata. The Upper Derwent and its tributaries flow mostly through shale and gritstone. Forests planted around the Derwent Reservoirs are a major feature and offer homes to woodland birds and a few deer as well as the smaller carnivorous animals. In the limestone dales, trees were once cut down for fuel but they are plentiful today and, in some instances, they are crowding other plant life. In Dove Dale, a courageous scheme has removed much of the invasive woodland to recreate more open vistas. Plant life on the craggy scree-covered hillsides is mostly dwarf and with an almost alpine quality.

But the dales are best known for their trout streams. Not only do game fish breed in their clear waters, but crayfish, a crustacean which needs pure water, is found beneath the rocks of most of the rivers in the dales.

10 LONG DISTANCE WALKS IN THE PEAK

Cal–Derwent Walk: a high level moorland route linking the Calder and Derwent valleys.
Derbyshire Gritstone Way: follows gritstone edges above the River Derwent from Edale to Derby.
Gritstone Trail: waymarked route along the western edge of the Peak District from Lyme Park to Mow Cop near Rudyard Lake where it links with the Staffordshire Way.
Limestone Way: a route waymarked with the 'Derby Ram' symbol from Matlock to Castleton across the limestone uplands.
The Pennine Way: Britain's first long distance footpath starts at Edale and follows a high level route along the Pennines to finish at Kirk Yetholm in Scotland.
The White Peak Way: a circular walk around the southern half of the Peak National Park. Easily divides into seven stages based on Bakewell, Elton, Ilam Hall, Hartington, Ravenstor, Castleton and Hathersage youth hostels.

Trails based on disused railways

High Peak Trail: follows the High Peak Railway (including Cromford Incline) from Cromford Wharf to Sparklow. Cycle hire scheme.
Manifold Valley Trail: Macadam surfaced track of the Manifold Valley Light Railway from Hulme End to Waterhouses. Suitable for wheel chairs but please note that sections are used by motorised traffic. Cycle hire scheme.
Monsal Trail: starts at Bakewell station and follows the Midland Line to Miller's Dale. Diverges to avoid tunnels. Spectacular scenic views of Monsal Dale. Cycle hire scheme.
Sett Valley Trail: Hayfield to New Mills cycle trackway with linking footpaths.

Tissington Trail: uses part of the Ashbourne to Buxton line to link with the High Peak Trail at Parsley Hay. Cycle hire scheme.

11 USEFUL ADDRESSES

Peak District National Park,
Aldern House,
Baslow Road,
BAKEWELL DE4 1AE,
Derbyshire. (Tel: Bakewell 4321)

Peak National Park Study Centre,
Losehill Hall,
CASTLETON S30 2WB,
Derbyshire. (Tel: Hope Valley 20373)

Bakewell Information Centre,
Old Market Hall,
BAKEWELL. (Tel: Bakewell 3227)

Buxton Information Centre,
The Crescent,
BUXTON. (Tel: Buxton 5106)

Castleton Information Centre,
Castles Street,
CASTLETON. (Tel: Hope Valley 20679)

Edale Information Centre,
Field Head,
EDALE. (Tel: Hope Valley 70207)

Ilam Hall National Trust Information Centre,
ILAM, Nr. Ashbourne. (Tel: Thorpe Cloud 245)

Matlock Bath Information Centre,
The Pavilion,
MATLOCK BATH. (Tel: Matlock 55082)

Temporary information centres are open at weekends and bank holidays throughout the summer months at:

Derbyshire Bridge (Goyt Valley)
Hartington Railway Station (Tissington Trail)
Tideswell Dale Picnic Site

Local and regional tourist offices can also be found at Ashbourne, Chesterfield, Leek, Macclesfield and Sheffield.

Walk 1
DERWENT MOORS
4¾ miles (7.6km) Easy/moderate; 550ft (168m) ascent

Here is a chance to experience the Derwent moors and edges at close hand. Both the wide footpath from Cutthroat Bridge and the second, which it joins near Moscar House, are easy to follow and use routes which predate the busy A57 road by many centuries. An airy track crosses the rocky escarpment of Derwent Edge where there are enticing views of the wild moors beyond Lady-bower. Dropping down through a mature pine forest, the final leg of the route conveniently passes the welcome sight of the Lady-bower Inn.

3 *Turn left along the crest of the rocky moorland escarpment.*

2 *Turn sharp left as directed by the footpath signpost. Beyond the upper wall, the path crosses the moor, following a line of shooting butts.*

4 *Turn right and go down the hillside. Follow the tracks to the left of the boundary wall, through mature pine forest.*

Derwent Moors

Grouse Butts

Grouse Butts

5 *Leave the forest and bear left, above a group of farm buildings, and go through two gates.*

Highshaw Clough

Ⓐ

Hurkling Stones

Ⓔ

🅿

Cutthroat Bridge

Ⓑ

Ⓓ

Ladybower Wood

1 *From the car park, walk down the road, then turn right on the rocky path. Turn sharp right beneath power lines. Cross the stream and follow a grassy path across the moor.*

Ashopton

Ⓒ

PH

6 *Turn right for the Ladybower Inn, otherwise bear left at the footpath junction (return to this point if visiting the pub); climb the rocky path to the open moor.*

7 *Turn right at the footpath junction to rejoin the A57.*

A Viewpoint. 'Wheel Stones' or the 'Coach & Horses', are the first of a line of distinctive gritstone outcrops along Derwent Edge. It is possible to extend the walk to make a closer inspection of the outcrops.

B Viewpoint looking across the northern arm of Ladybower Reservoir.

C Ladybower Woods is a nature reserve owned and cared for by the Derbyshire Naturalist Trust.

D Viewpoint. Look back at the surprise view of the lower section of Ladybower Reservoir.

E Cutthroat Bridge. The name commemorates a gruesome murder on this spot in 1635.

Walk 2
LADYBOWER
6½ miles (10.5km) Moderate; one 580ft (177m) climb

Here is a walk with contrasting views. Starting near the Ashopton viaduct, it leaves the reservoir by climbing steadily across the flank of Crook Hill along an ancient bridleway. This track carried people and goods between West Yorkshire and Cheshire, long before the Snake Road turnpike was built. The views from Crook Hill, especially those opposite, of the edges above the Derwent Valley, are most spectacular. Strange rock formations with fanciful names dot the eastern skyline and the eye is carried easily across the heights from scene to scene. Quiet forest glades lead down to the man-made lake of Ladybower where a quiet road is followed along its eastern shore, to the busy A57.

During summer weekends and bank holidays, the road from Fairholmes to the dale head is free of all but essential motor traffic. A mini bus service carries pedestrians to various points along the road and a cycle hire scheme helps visitors enjoy the tranquillity and beauty of this secluded valley.

A Crook Hill viewpoint. To the east, across the deep cleft of flooded Derwent Dale, the eastern skyline is marked by rocky outcrops, more in keeping with Dartmoor Tors. Most of the rocks are named but two, in particular, should be obvious from their shape, even at this distance: one is the 'Salt Cellar' and the other, the 'Coach & Horses' (marked 'Wheel Stones' on the OS map), is just like a 19th-century mail coach. Even though it is man-made and completely altered the appearance of the dale, Ladybower Reservoir makes an attractive contrast to the wild moors beyond.

Westward from Crook Hill and across the Woodlands Valley arm of the reservoir, are the heights of Win Hill and Kinder Scout.

B Viewpoint. Kinder Scout's northern edges dominate the Ashop Valley and over the northern shoulder of Win Hill, Mam Tor's undulating ridge marks the boundary between the Dark and White Peak. To the north, the underlying rocks were laid down by an ancient river delta millions of years ago. The river in its turn buried the even older limestone, deposited by countless sea creatures in a tropical sea.

C Viewpoint. From the farm look across Lockerbrook Plantation to Ladybower Reservoir and the Derwent Edges.

D Derwent Dam. When the reservoir is full, water cascades over the dam wall creating the largest waterfall in the Peak. The dam was used by members of the famous Dam Busters Squadron, when they were training for the wartime raids on the Möhne and Eder dams in the Ruhr. The same dam was used in the film portraying this courageous exploit.

E A plaque at the side of the Mill Brook tells the sad story of the lost village of Derwent. All that remains of this village is the re-erected war memorial on the roadside above the west shore of the reservoir. A graceful pack-horse bridge, which was sited near the village, now crosses the River Derwent at Slippery Stones almost at the head of the valley.

F There is another drowned village below this point. This was Ashopton, once reached by a steep tree-shrouded lane below the A57. It is hard to imagine, gazing out over millions of gallons of water, that the Derwent flowed past Ashopton on its way south through a deep rocky valley. All that tranquillity ended in 1943, when the sluices were shut and water drowned an idyllic valley with its farms and villages.

Over

12

Walk 2
Ladybower
continued

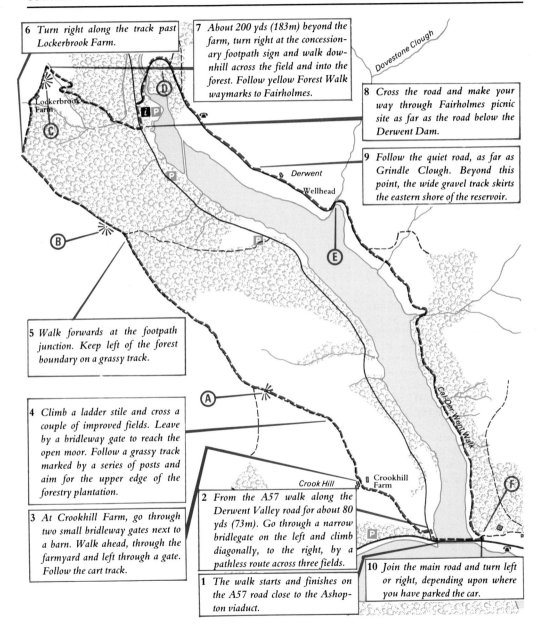

6 Turn right along the track past Lockerbrook Farm.

7 About 200 yds (183m) beyond the farm, turn right at the concessionary footpath sign and walk downhill across the field and into the forest. Follow yellow Forest Walk waymarks to Fairholmes.

8 Cross the road and make your way through Fairholmes picnic site as far as the road below the Derwent Dam.

9 Follow the quiet road, as far as Grindle Clough. Beyond this point, the wide gravel track skirts the eastern shore of the reservoir.

5 Walk forwards at the footpath junction. Keep left of the forest boundary on a grassy track.

4 Climb a ladder stile and cross a couple of improved fields. Leave by a bridleway gate to reach the open moor. Follow a grassy track marked by a series of posts and aim for the upper edge of the forestry plantation.

3 At Crookhill Farm, go through two small bridleway gates next to a barn. Walk ahead, through the farmyard and left through a gate. Follow the cart track.

2 From the A57 walk along the Derwent Valley road for about 80 yds (73m). Go through a narrow bridlegate on the left and climb diagonally, to the right, by a pathless route across three fields.

1 The walk starts and finishes on the A57 road close to the Ashopton viaduct.

10 Join the main road and turn left or right, depending upon where you have parked the car.

Dovestone Clough

Lockerbrook Farm

Derwent

Wellhead

Crook Hill

Crookhill Farm

Calder Wean Walk

WIN HILL

5 miles (8km) Strenuous; one 966ft (294m) climb

0 ─────────────────────── 1 mile
0 ─────────────────── 1 km

Access to the start of this walk is along the Thornhill road from Yorkshire Bridge village. There is limited parking and so try not to inconvenience anyone.

After a steep initial climb, fortunately the one and only climb on the walk, the views from Win Hill summit offer an ample reward. From then on the walking is easy, level or downhill back to Yorkshire Bridge, with the path along the shore of Ladybower Reservoir, making a pleasing contrast to the moors above.

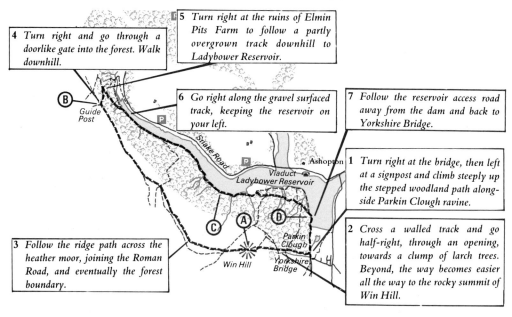

4 *Turn right and go through a doorlike gate into the forest. Walk downhill.*

5 *Turn right at the ruins of Elmin Pits Farm to follow a partly overgrown track downhill to Ladybower Reservoir.*

6 *Go right along the gravel surfaced track, keeping the reservoir on your left.*

7 *Follow the reservoir access road away from the dam and back to Yorkshire Bridge.*

1 *Turn right at the bridge, then left at a signpost and climb steeply up the stepped woodland path alongside Parkin Clough ravine.*

2 *Cross a walled track and go half-right, through an opening, towards a clump of larch trees. Beyond, the way becomes easier all the way to the rocky summit of Win Hill.*

3 *Follow the ridge path across the heather moor, joining the Roman Road, and eventually the forest boundary.*

B Guide Post

Snake Road

Ashopton

Viaduct
Ladybower Reservoir

Parkin Clough

Win Hill

Yorkshire Bridge

A Viewpoint. The all-round view takes in the Dark and much of the White Peak. The name Win Hill is supposed to commemorate a battle between two rival chieftains in 632. The winners camped here and the losers across the valley on Lose Hill. This is the romantic story but a more mundane explanation is that Win is a shortened version of 'whin' or 'gorse', and Lose, especially with its local pronunciation, 'loose' describes the nature of the underlying shale.

B Guide Post. This old stone marker was erected in 1737 to show the way to travellers either on foot or on horseback.

C Viewpoint. The sound of traffic crossing the Ashopton Viaduct on the far side of the reservoir does not intrude upon this quiet woodland setting. The only sounds are from woodland birds and water fowl.

D Ladybower Dam. Two eerie looking circular overflow pits take the excess water of this last of three reservoirs filling the Upper Derwent. Finished in 1943, Ladybower Reservoir drowned the picturesque villages of Ashopton and Derwent further up the valley. Most of their inhabitants were rehoused in an estate specially built for them in Yorkshire Bridge.

Sheep dog trials are a popular event in nearby Bamford. Every Spring Bank Holiday Monday, competitors come to the valley from all over the country.

GRINDSBROOK SKYLINE

5½ miles (8.8km) Strenuous; attempt only in fine weather; one 1210ft (369m) climb

Generations of walkers and climbers have approached Kinder Scout from Edale. On the moorland edge, gritstone rocks worn by wind and weather, are reminiscent of sculptures by Henry Moore.

The Pennine Way has its southern portal in Edale and many hopeful walkers have had or abandon their attempt right at the start because they were ill-prepared for the hazards of Kinder. **Never attempt this walk in bad weather or mist.**

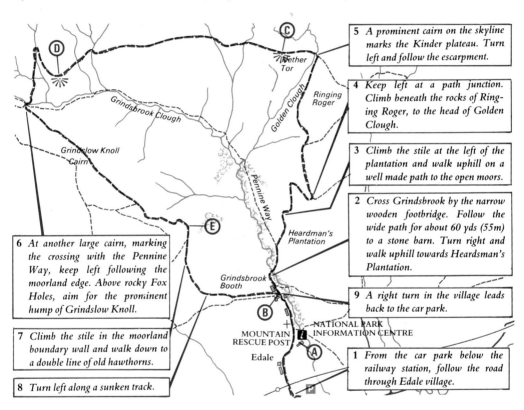

5 *A prominent cairn on the skyline marks the Kinder plateau. Turn left and follow the escarpment.*

4 *Keep left at a path junction. Climb beneath the rocks of Ringing Roger, to the head of Golden Clough.*

3 *Climb the stile at the left of the plantation and walk uphill on a well made path to the open moors.*

2 *Cross Grindsbrook by the narrow wooden footbridge. Follow the wide path for about 60 yds (55m) to a stone barn. Turn right and walk uphill towards Heardsman's Plantation.*

6 *At another large cairn, marking the crossing with the Pennine Way, keep left following the moorland edge. Above rocky Fox Holes, aim for the prominent hump of Grindslow Knoll.*

9 *A right turn in the village leads back to the car park.*

7 *Climb the stile in the moorland boundary wall and walk down to a double line of old hawthorns.*

1 *From the car park below the railway station, follow the road through Edale village.*

8 *Turn left along a sunken track.*

A Field Head, the Peak District National Park Information Centre. Call in to check the weather forecast and leave a note of your intended route.

B The Pennine Way starts by the Nags Head Inn.

C Viewpoint. From the weather worn rocks of Nether Tor, across the valley to Rushup Edge (right) and Mam Tor (left).

D Viewpoint. Below is Grindsbrook. Deep tortuously winding channels in the peat of Kinder are known as 'groughs'.

E Where the path enters a shallow groove below Grindslow Knoll, it follows the line of an old sledge track, made to drag peat from the moor.

Walk 5
BROWN KNOLL
6¼ miles (10km) Moderate/Strenuous; 1103ft (336m) climb

This walk starts from Kinder road quarry — a place with important historical connections in the struggle for public access to open spaces. A plaque commemorates the mass trespass over Kinder Scout on 24th April 1932. Its ringleaders were given harsh jail sentences but the seeds were sown, eventually giving us the precious right to roam across many of our wild open spaces — a right which is exercised on the moorland section of this walk.

5 Go through a kissing gate and climb, half right, on a prominent path.

4 Cross the 'in-by' grazing, climbing stiles in the boundary walls.

3 Pass to the right of the farm buildings, then left uphill along a walled track.

2 Turn left, away from the river, through the gate marked Tunstead House and follow the access drive uphill.

1 Cross the bridge opposite the car park and turn left along the valley road following the River Sett.

13 Go left on the metalled track. Follow it down the valley and back to the quarry car park.

6 Cross a wooden stile in the boundary wall and turn left to follow the rough track.

12 Turn right through a metal gate and along the grassy path over the broad col. Walk downhill to the left, across the steep hillside.

7 Turn right in front of the gate and away from the stoney track. Follow the wall and fence across Brown Knoll Moor.

8 Ignoring stiles in the fence, continue to follow the often faint path around the head-waters of the River Sett.

9 Keep to the right of a complex wall junction and aim towards the prominent bulk of South Head.

10 Turn right, along the wide rutted track, ignoring a faint signposted path descending further to the right. Follow the track round the left flank of Mount Famine.

11 Downhill following along the walled track towards a corregated farm shelter.

Map labels: Crowden Tower; Noe Stool; Edale Rocks; Brown Knoll; Edale Cross; River Sett; South Head; Coldwell Clough; Mount Famine; Tunstead Clough Farm; Kinder Road

A Viewpoint of the upper Sett Valley looking towards the twin hills of Mount Famine and South Head.

B Viewpoint. The hill on the left is Kinder Low, the south western outlier of Kinder Scout.

C Edale Cross marked the boundary of the monastic lands of Basingwerk Abbey (near Holywell in Flintshire).

D Viewpoint across the headwaters of the Vale of Edale looking towards rocky outcrops.

E Viewpoint. The western rim of Kinder Scout rises above the pastures of Sett Valley farms. In wet weather and with a strong westerly wind, the Kinder river is thrown backwards in a huge plume from the Downfall.

Walk 6
RUSHUP EDGE
5½ miles (8.8km) Moderate; one 1029ft (314m) climb

0 ——————————————— 1 mile
0 ——————————— 1 km

The climb to reach the summit of Rushup Edge is amply rewarded with superb views. In the north the gritstone plateau of Kinder Scout rises menacingly above Edale but, to the south, the White Peak and its limestone based pasture is far gentler. The boundary between these geological contrasts is followed by the A625 road at the foot of Rushup Edge.

4 Cross the bridge and turn right along the minor road.

3 Turn right through the hamlet of Barber Booth and right again at the valley road.

1 Walk towards Edale village. Beyond the police houses, turn left over a stile and follow the waymarked route across three fields.

5 Climb the stile on the left and follow a field path.

6 Using stiles, keep well to the right of the outbuildings of Manor House farm. Cross a series of fields by lining up stiles.

7 At the moorland boundary, turn right at the path junction and follow the old sunken track, known as Chapel Gate, steeply uphill to the high moors.

2 Keep left of Shaw Wood Farm. Following the yellow waymark arrows, cross the drive and walk diagonally across the next field. Continue, parallel to the railway. Go through a kissing gate and left over the railway bridge.

12 Keep right of the house and follow its access lane, at the side of Harden Clough, back to Edale.

8 Bear half left at the signposted path junction and continue across the moor.

11 Go through the wicket gate on the right and immediately turn left, downhill on a broad track.

9 Turn left at the signpost to follow the broad, sandy path along the ridge of Rushup Edge.

10 Climb steeply to the road and turn left.

Map labels: Grindslow House, Grindsbrook Booth, Ollerbrook Booth, NATIONAL PARK INFORMATION CENTRE, MOUNTAIN RESCUE POST, Edale, Shaw Woods, Barber Booth, Manor House Farm, Chapel Gate (Track), Rushup Edge, Eldon Hill Quarries, Blue John Cavern, (A) (B) (C) (D)

A Call in at the Fieldhead National Park Information Centre to get the local weather forecast.

B Viewpoint. To the southwest, Combs Moss rises above Chapel-en-le-Frith. Beyond, the limestone plateau of White Peak.

C Viewpoint. Lord's Seat Tumulus. To the north, rocky outcrops on Kinder Scout stand out from the stark moor. In contrast to the south, the panorama is totally limestone.

D Viewpoint. The ramparts of a prehistoric fort stand out sharply on Mam Tor.

E Shales lining Mam Nick are as those which cause the slipping of Mam Tor's south face.

Walk 7
STANAGE EDGE
7 miles (11.3km) Easy/Moderate; 914ft (279m) climb

This is a walk steeped in romantic legend; Robin Hood's henchman, Little John, is reputed to be buried in Hathersage churchyard and the hero of Sherwood, had an almost inaccessible refuge in a cave on Stanage Edge. The long, dramatic escarpment, where rock climbers can be seen practicing their skillful moves, has been scaled by climbers since the 1890s and has over 500 routes of varying technical difficulty. High Lees Hall, lying in a sunny sheltered valley below the rocks, featured in Charlotte Brönte's romantic novel, *Jane Eyre*.

Millstones litter the slopes below Stanage Edge. Now used as symbolic boundary markers of the Peak National Park, they were once in great demand for making woodpulp.

A Hathersage church. Little John's grave is opposite the main door. St Michael's church was built in the 14th and 15th centuries but it lies within the circular mound of a religion pre-dating Christianity.

B Viewpoint looking uphill over the moors towards the rocky escarpment of Stanage Edge.

C Viewpoint. Hope Valley is to the far right with Eyam Moor to the left.

D Viewpoint looking down to the enigmatic rocks of Carl Wark Fort on the right of a plantation of mixed conifers. Burbage Rocks line the left upper rim of the valley.

E Viewpoint. This is one of the finest views in the Peak. The Derwent Edges reach towards the horizon and Rushup Edge, Win Hill, Kinder Scout and Bleaklow can be seen across the valley.

Southward, the view encompasses most of the uplands of the White Peak where clumps of trees on hilltops indicate ancient burial mounds. Millstones littering the foot of Stanage Edge were carved by stone-masons who then left them until required by the Scandinavian wood pulp industry. This trade died when longer-lasting steel rollers took over. The typical 'wheel' shape of these stones with flat outer rims, indicates their use as grindstones. Stones used for flour milling are usually bevelled.

F Robin Hood's Cave. This draughty opening in the rocks could well have been used by a local bandit in less settled times but it is unknown how this cave, and a well on nearby Longshaw Estate, came by the title.

G Viewpoint looking uphill towards the crags of Stanage Edge. The path at this point was once part of a pack horse way, an important link between Sheffield and Manchester.

H North Lees Hall. This three storied, semi-fortified manor house is something of a rarity so far south. It is similar in purpose to the pele towers of the Scottish Borders offering protection to owners in the upper storeys and their animals on the ground floor.

North Lees and its estate now cared for by the Peak National Park, for many generations was owned by the Eyre family, who were recorded amongst the bowmen at Agincourt.

Charlotte Brönte stayed at Hathersage Vicarage for three weeks in 1845 with her friend Ellen Massey and her novel *Jane Eyre* came as a result of that holiday. Many of the settings used in the story can be recognised as places around Hathersage. North Lees Hall is clearly identified as Thornfield Hall from which Jane fled.

Over

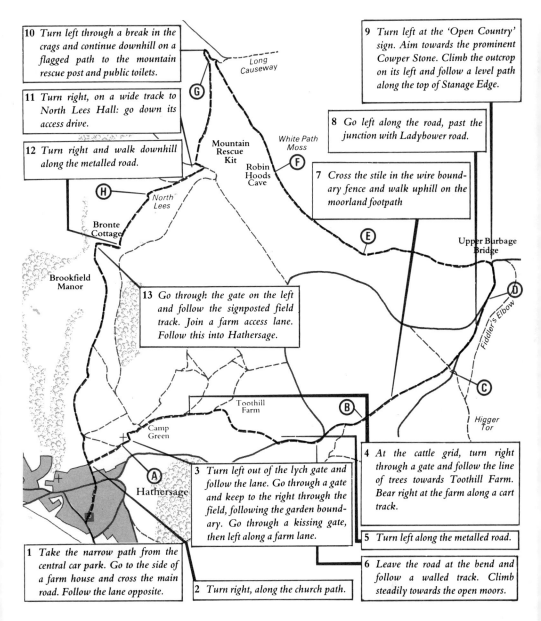

0   1 mile
0   1 km

10 Turn left through a break in the crags and continue downhill on a flagged path to the mountain rescue post and public toilets.

11 Turn right, on a wide track to North Lees Hall: go down its access drive.

12 Turn right and walk downhill along the metalled road.

9 Turn left at the 'Open Country' sign. Aim towards the prominent Cowper Stone. Climb the outcrop on its left and follow a level path along the top of Stanage Edge.

8 Go left along the road, past the junction with Ladybower road.

7 Cross the stile in the wire boundary fence and walk uphill on the moorland footpath

13 Go through the gate on the left and follow the signposted field track. Join a farm access lane. Follow this into Hathersage.

4 At the cattle grid, turn right through a gate and follow the line of trees towards Toothill Farm. Bear right at the farm along a cart track.

3 Turn left out of the lych gate and follow the lane. Go through a gate and keep to the right through the field, following the garden boundary. Go through a kissing gate, then left along a farm lane.

5 Turn left along the metalled road.

1 Take the narrow path from the central car park. Go to the side of a farm house and cross the main road. Follow the lane opposite.

2 Turn right, along the church path.

6 Leave the road at the bend and follow a walled track. Climb steadily towards the open moors.

Map labels:
Long Causeway · White Path Moss · Mountain Rescue Kit · Robin Hoods Cave · North Lees · Bronte Cottage · Brookfield Manor · Upper Burbage Bridge · Fiddler's Elbow · Toothill Farm · Higger Tor · Camp Green · Hathersage

G · F · E · H · D · C · B · A

Walk 8
CASTLETON
6 miles (9.6km) Moderate/Strenuous; total ascent: 1095ft (334m)

Castleton is popular with thousands of visitors who come each year to visit its caves, climb the steep slope of the castle or simply to enjoy the local scenery. This walk leaves Castleton by an almost hidden route and climbs to the limestone uplands along the bed of a collapsed cave. Mam Tor dramatically marks the change from limestone to the gritstone and shales of the Dark Peak. Iron Age man built a refuge on 'Shivering Mountain' and his prodigious workmanship can still be traced by lines of complex defensive ditches.

A St Edmund's, Castleton's Parish Church, has a unique collection of Bibles, including a Cranmer Bible of 1539 and a 'Breeches' Bible of 1611.

B Castleton's castle was built in 1080 by William Peveril, son of the Conqueror, as a wooden stockade. The present stone Keep dates from 1176, when it cost £135! To the right of the castle, the mouth of Peak Cavern and then, on the left, Cave Dale's natural walls complete the ideal defenses situation.

Castleton has two special events each year: the first is Garland Day held during the evening of 29th May to celebrate the restoration of the Monarchy. The "garland" is a large wood-framed cone covered with flowers which fits over the head and shoulders of the 'king'. Dressed in Jacobean costume, a king and queen ride through the village accompanied by the local band and dancing children. The garland is hoisted to the top of the church tower and left until all the flowers have died. Every Christmas the village is decorated with dozens of illuminated Christmas trees.

C Beyond the iron gate at the top of the dale, there is a small outcrop of dull brown rock to the left. This is dolerite, a form of basalt.

D The round shallow pond on the right of the path is manmade, to hold rainwater on the dry limestone uplands.

E Windy Knoll. The shallow depression has yielded fascinating relics to both geologists and palaeontologists. Bitumen exuding from the rocks hints that there was probably an infant oil field in the vicinity. In 1870 Bone Cave yielded up the remains of a sabre toothed tiger and grisly bear.

F Mam Tor. The massive earthworks of the Iron Age Fort here can still be traced.

G The view from the summit takes in Kinder Scout and the Edale Valley to the north and, to the southeast, you can see the Hope Valley and Castleton. The White and Dark Peak meet here. Mam Tor is made from unstable mud and grit shales. The locals call it the Shivering Mountain. Land-slip has led to the abandonment of the A625 at the foot of the hill.

The partly natural caverns of Blue John, Speedwell and Treak Cliff are open to the public.

Beyond the A625 is Treak Cliff where lead was mined.

H Viewpoint. The entrance to the Winnats (Wind Gates) can be seen to the left of Treak Cliff.

In 1758 an eloping couple hoping to reach Peak Forest, were murdered by miners in the Winnats and their bodies thrown down a shaft. Although none of the murderers came to justice, they all met violent deaths except one who confessed on his deathbed.

Over

0   1 mile
0   1 km

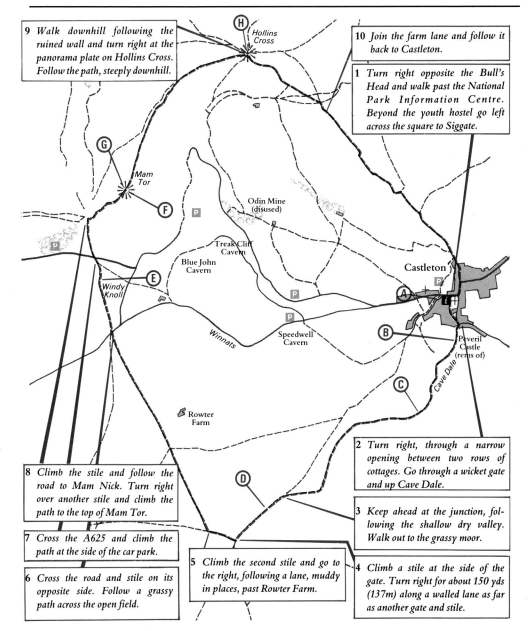

9 *Walk downhill following the ruined wall and turn right at the panorama plate on Hollins Cross. Follow the path, steeply downhill.*

10 *Join the farm lane and follow it back to Castleton.*

1 *Turn right opposite the Bull's Head and walk past the National Park Information Centre. Beyond the youth hostel go left across the square to Siggate.*

Hollins Cross

Mam Tor

Odin Mine (disused)

Treak Cliff Cavern

Blue John Cavern

Windy Knoll

Castleton

Winnats

Speedwell Cavern

Peveril Castle (rems of)

Cave Dale

Rowter Farm

8 *Climb the stile and follow the road to Mam Nick. Turn right over another stile and climb the path to the top of Mam Tor.*

7 *Cross the A625 and climb the path at the side of the car park.*

6 *Cross the road and stile on its opposite side. Follow a grassy path across the open field.*

5 *Climb the second stile and go to the right, following a lane, muddy in places, past Rowter Farm.*

2 *Turn right, through a narrow opening between two rows of cottages. Go through a wicket gate and up Cave Dale.*

3 *Keep ahead at the junction, following the shallow dry valley. Walk out to the grassy moor.*

4 *Climb a stile at the side of the gate. Turn right for about 150 yds (137m) along a walled lane as far as another gate and stile.*

Walk 9
LYME PARK AND SPONDS HILL
5 miles (8km) Easy/Moderate; one 478ft (146m) climb

Lyme Hall was the home of the Legh family for many generations but death duties and running costs forced them to relinquish this fine Palladian house and its deer park.

This is a popular walk which offers unrivalled views of the house and its formal grounds and then climbs to open breezy moorland heights.

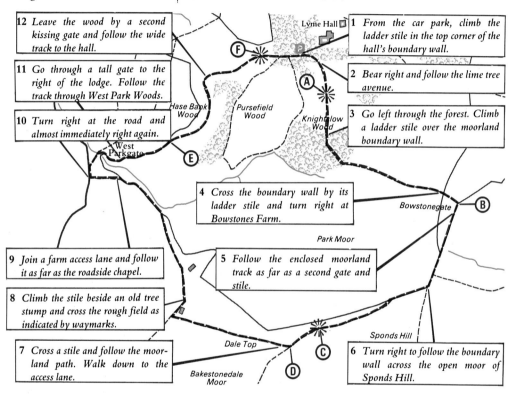

12 Leave the wood by a second kissing gate and follow the wide track to the hall.

11 Go through a tall gate to the right of the lodge. Follow the track through West Park Woods.

10 Turn right at the road and almost immediately right again.

9 Join a farm access lane and follow it as far as the roadside chapel.

8 Climb the stile beside an old tree stump and cross the rough field as indicated by waymarks.

7 Cross a stile and follow the moorland path. Walk down to the access lane.

1 From the car park, climb the ladder stile in the top corner of the hall's boundary wall.

2 Bear right and follow the lime tree avenue.

3 Go left through the forest. Climb a ladder stile over the moorland boundary wall.

4 Cross the boundary wall by its ladder stile and turn right at Bowstones Farm.

5 Follow the enclosed moorland track as far as a second gate and stile.

6 Turn right to follow the boundary wall across the open moor of Sponds Hill.

Lyme Hall
Hase Bank Wood
Pursefield Wood
Knightlow Wood
West Parkgate
Park Moor
Bowstonegate
Sponds Hill
Dale Top
Bakestonedale Moor

A View of Lyme Hall across its ornamental lake.

B Bowstones. These are the two stone pillars enclosed by a low metal fence near the farm entrance. The name suggests that they might have been used in the making of bows but they probably predate these weapons.

C Viewpoint. Lyme Hall can be seen beyond its surrounding pine woods.

D The hollows on Dale Top were once shallow coal pits.

E In May and June rhododendrons make a contrasting splash of pink and red against the dark green of the pines.

F Viewpoint. The Palladian frontage of Lyme Hall is seen to its best advantage here. The Dutch garden is worth closer examination, especially in the late spring when the tulips are in full bloom.

Walk 10
COMBS

4 miles (6.4km) Moderate; muddy sections

The walk starts and finishes at the pleasant village of Combs, which moorland of Combs Moss, a little Beehive Inn, a focal point of the nestles snugly beneath the wild known outlier of the Dark Peak.

1 Follow the Dove Holes road away from the front of the Beehive Inn.

2 Where the road bears left, turn right along a lane through Rye Flatt farmyard.

3 A few yards beyond a modern bungalow and where the lane bears left to Allstone Lee Farm, continue ahead, over a stile and along a field path signposted to White Hall.

4 Cross two adjacent footbridges, one stone, the other plank. Climb a series of fields using stiles and gateways to keep on course.

5 Turn sharp right through Combshead farmyard, go through a gateway and turn left, uphill, beside a wire fence above a shallow gully. Keep to the pathless route by using stiles in field boundaries.

6 Cross a stile and turn right on to a moorland road, then right again beyond the hall. Keep left at a road junction after another 250 yds (229m).

7 Turn right opposite the modernised farmhouse of Wainstones. Go past a ruined barn and out along the rough field track beneath a stony ridge.

8 After crossing three rough fields, bear right downhill to a walled lane. Follow it left to Haylee Farm. Go right, through the farmyard and left along a leafy lane.

9 Turn right at the lane end and follow the road back to the village.

A Viewpoint. The private grouse moor of Combs Moss is in front. To the left are the crags of Castle Naze, a favourite training ground for local rock climbers. Behind the rocks and out of sight, a solid earthen bank marks the limits of an Iron Age fort.

B Viewpoint. The slopes below the building on the skyline to the left are covered by bracken which will not grow on the windy heights beyond the moorland edge. That region is given over to heather and bilberry.

C White Hall is an Outdoor Pursuits Centre run by Derbyshire County Council.

D The road follows the route between Roman Arnemetia (Buxton) and Mancunium (Manchester).

E Viewpoint. Combs village fits snugly in a wide hollow beneath its Moss. In the distance, to your half left, is Kinder Scout and its outliers.

23

Walk 11
PEAK FOREST
4¼ miles (6.8km) Easy

0   1 mile

0   1 km

Lands of the northern Peak were once a royal hunting preserve, or forest, controlled by harsh laws. Cruel punishments were inflicted on anyone other than the nobility who was caught taking the King's game. Today the only link with the past is the name of the village, Peak Forest — a scattering of farms and sturdy cottages, fortunately neglected by motorists hurrying along the A623. Peak Forest once had a certain notoriety when it became a kind of English Gretna Green, permitting eloping couples to marry in its parish church.

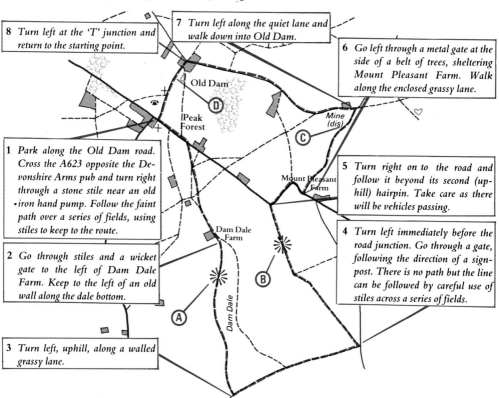

8 Turn left at the 'T' junction and return to the starting point.

7 Turn left along the quiet lane and walk down into Old Dam.

6 Go left through a metal gate at the side of a belt of trees, sheltering Mount Pleasant Farm. Walk along the enclosed grassy lane.

1 Park along the Old Dam road. Cross the A623 opposite the Devonshire Arms pub and turn right through a stone stile near an old iron hand pump. Follow the faint path over a series of fields, using stiles to keep to the route.

2 Go through stiles and a wicket gate to the left of Dam Dale Farm. Keep to the left of an old wall along the dale bottom.

3 Turn left, uphill, along a walled grassy lane.

5 Turn right on to the road and follow it beyond its second (uphill) hairpin. Take care as there will be vehicles passing.

4 Turn left immediately before the road junction. Go through a gate, following the direction of a signpost. There is no path but the line can be followed by careful use of stiles across a series of fields.

Map labels: Old Dam, Peak Forest, Mine (dis), Mount Pleasant Farm, Dam Dale Farm, Dam Dale, and points A, B, C, D.

A Viewpoint. Dam Dale — a typical upland limestone dale where the plant life is more closely related to an alpine environment.

B Viewpoint. Peak Forest lies in the hollow below Eldon Hill.

Rushup Edge is in the background, marking the division between the southerly limestones and gritstone of the Dark Peak.

C Humps and hollows in the open space at the lane end denote one-time lead mining in the area.

A nearby cottage usually offers refreshments.

D The duck pond on the left was a man-made communal watering place for village cattle in the days before piped water reached the surrounding farms.

Walk 12
SHATTON MOOR

4½ miles (7.2km) Easy; one 775ft (236m) climb

Quiet lanes climb the windswept heights to moors which offer unrivalled views across the southern boundary of the Dark Peak. This easy walk covers a part of the Peak which is often neglected by walkers. An added attraction is the opportunity to watch gliders from nearby Hucklow Edge seeking updrafts along the heights. Gliders are the only manmade intrusion in this area of solitude.

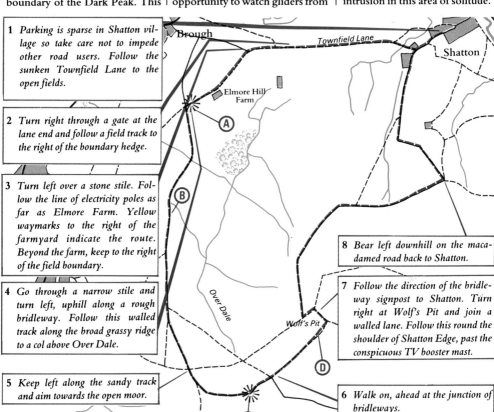

1 *Parking is sparse in Shatton village so take care not to impede other road users. Follow the sunken Townfield Lane to the open fields.*

2 *Turn right through a gate at the lane end and follow a field track to the right of the boundary hedge.*

3 *Turn left over a stone stile. Follow the line of electricity poles as far as Elmore Farm. Yellow waymarks to the right of the farmyard indicate the route. Beyond the farm, keep to the right of the field boundary.*

4 *Go through a narrow stile and turn left, uphill along a rough bridleway. Follow this walled track along the broad grassy ridge to a col above Over Dale.*

5 *Keep left along the sandy track and aim towards the open moor.*

6 *Walk on, ahead at the junction of bridleways.*

7 *Follow the direction of the bridleway signpost to Shatton. Turn right at Wolf's Pit and join a walled lane. Follow this round the shoulder of Shatton Edge, past the conspicuous TV booster mast.*

8 *Bear left downhill on the macadamed road back to Shatton.*

A The view of the Edale Valley and Mam Tor Ridge is only marred by the intrusive chimney of the cement works.

B Grey Ditch and Rebellion Knoll. The prominent earth-work on the right of the track reaches down to Bradwell. This is an ancient boundary but its links with Rebellion Knoll, the small rise beyond Grey Ditch, are unclear. It could refer to a rebellion of slaves in the Roman lead mines. There was an administrative fort at Navio, near Brough.

C Viewpoint. Bretton Clough ('home of the Britons') is to the south.

D Viewpoint. Over Dale Nature Reserve fills the valley head and is the haunt of moorland birds.

Walk 13
EYAM MOOR
4¾ miles (7.6km) Moderate

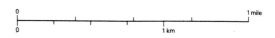

The wildest moors in the Peak District lie north of a rough crescent drawn from Leek through Buxton to Sheffield. Southwards, and often isolated as outliers within the limestone uplands, are areas of gentler heather-clad moors. This walk crosses one of them. Eyam Moor is an exhilarating place with the deep wooded confines of Highlow Brook making an interesting contrast.

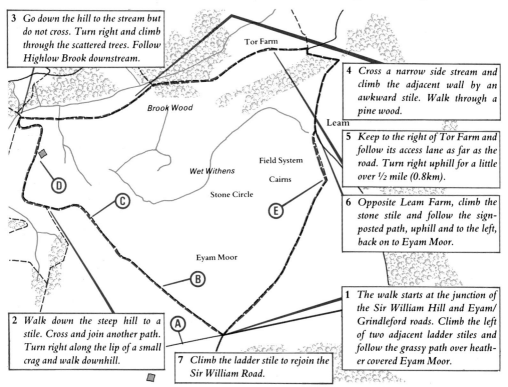

3 Go down the hill to the stream but do not cross. Turn right and climb through the scattered trees. Follow Highlow Brook downstream.

Tor Farm

4 Cross a narrow side stream and climb the adjacent wall by an awkward stile. Walk through a pine wood.

Brook Wood

Leam

5 Keep to the right of Tor Farm and follow its access lane as far as the road. Turn right uphill for a little over ½ mile (0.8km).

Field System

Wet Withens

Cairns

Stone Circle

Ⓓ

Ⓒ

Ⓔ

6 Opposite Leam Farm, climb the stone stile and follow the signposted path, uphill and to the left, back on to Eyam Moor.

Eyam Moor

Ⓑ

1 The walk starts at the junction of the Sir William Hill and Eyam/Grindleford roads. Climb the left of two adjacent ladder stiles and follow the grassy path over heather covered Eyam Moor.

2 Walk down the steep hill to a stile. Cross and join another path. Turn right along the lip of a small crag and walk downhill.

Ⓐ

7 Climb the ladder stile to rejoin the Sir William Road.

A Sir William Road. The road was built in 1757 as part of the Manchester to Sheffield turnpike but who Sir William was is open to conjecture; one story relates to Sir William Cavendish, son of Bess of Hardwick, who fought for the King in the Civil War. Another suggestion is Sir William Saville, Lord of the Manor of Eyam and a third is Sir William Bagshawe, a local worthy.

B Burnt strips in the moorland heather are called 'swiddens' — an old Norse word. These strips are deliberate and encourage new growth which, in turn, provides food for the grouse.

C Viewpoint across Abney Clough to Offerton Moor.

D Viewpoint of wooded Abney Clough with Offerton Moor in the distance.

E Viewpoint. The Eastern Edges stretch in an almost unbroken line above the Derwent Valley. Enigmatic Cairns and hut circles in the heather of Eyam Moor are the remains of a civilisation which left no records.

Walk 14

CARL WARK AND HIGGER TOR

3¾ miles (6km) Easy/moderate; boggy sections

0			½ mile
0			1 km

There are many enigmas in the Peak District: stone circles, cairns and burial mounds were left by a community which had no means of conveying their purpose to us. Possibly of slightly later antiquity, Carl Wark hill fort hints of the need for tribes of the time to protect themselves from attack. We cannot tell whether this fort is Iron Age, or even post Roman, but what is certain is that it was built in such a way that even the siege of time has had little effect.

5 *Clamber across the summit rocks and follow the escarpment to the right. Follow the moorland path parallel to Fidler's Elbow road.*

6 *Cross the stream beneath Upper Burbage Bridge and climb its far bank to reach the road at a wooden stile. Turn right along the road for 100yds (91m).*

4 *Cross the low col beyond the fort and climb the wide peaty path towards the rocks of Higger Tor.*

7 *Go through the gate to the right of the road and follow the green track past a series of abandoned gritstone quarries as far as the main road.*

2 *Join the A625 at Burbage Bridge. Follow the road as far as the Toad's Mouth rock.*

3 *Cross the fence stile on the Hathersage side of the Toad's Mouth rock and follow an upward path across the moor, through heather and bracken. Aim for the prominent knoll of Carl Wark.*

8 *Turn left and follow the road if returning to the car park.*

1 *From the Longshaw Estate car park, walk through the narrow belt of beechwoods to the estate lodge. Cross the B6521 to enter a stretch of mixed woodland flanking the A625 below the Fox House Inn.*

Upper Burbage Bridge
Fiddler's Elbow
Higger Tor
Carl Wark
Burbage Bridge
Toad's Mouth
Fox House Inn
Longshaw Lodge

A Toad's Mouth. This rock stands at the side of the road. When viewed from below, the projecting snout and carved eye are said to resemble the head of a toad but you will not be alone if you feel that the likeness is closer to a moray eel!

B Carl Wark hill fort. The massive stone walls of the outer perimeter of this defensive point have stood the test of time. Traces of hut foundations and water troughs can still be seen. Notice also how the walls overshadow the two entrance points.

C Viewpoint. Carl Wark is below on its natural eminence with the Derwent Valley and heather clad moors stretching into the distance.

D Viewpoint. Burbage Brook follows its rocky way from its moorland birth. A plantation of mixed conifers adds to the pleasant scene.

Walk 15
PADLEY GORGE

0   1 mile

0   1 km

3¾ miles (6km) Moderate; 600ft (183m) descent and ascent

A deep rocky gorge, surrounded by ancient oak woodland, and a splendid Victorian hunting lodge screened by rhododendrons are the main features on this walk. The views are far ranging and yet contrast with the arboreal beauty of Padley Gorge.

If time and energies permit, this walk can be regarded as an extension to Walk number 14.

3 *Cross the stream by a log bridge and turn left, downstream.*

2 *Cross the road and follow the path down to Burbage Brook.*

4 *Go ahead at the path junction, walking down a steep hill through ancient oak woods lining Padley Gorge. Try to keep the stream in sight below and on the left, ignoring side turnings along this rocky woodland path.*

Robin Hood's Well

1 *From the Longshaw Estate car park, follow the woodland path to the estate lodge at the side of the B6521, Frogatt Road.*

Longshaw Lodge

10 *Go through a narrow gate to the left of Longshaw Lodge, follow the path around the foot of the 'ha-ha' back to the car park.*

Owler Tor

Lawrence Field

5 *Go through a kissing gate and down a rough lane past groups of houses. Turn left at the bottom and follow the lane over the railway bridge to a café.*

Settlement

Little John's Well

9 *Climb a ladder stile and turn left along the woodland drive. Follow this level track in and out of planted woodland and open grassland dotted by clumps of semi-wild rhododendrons.*

Longshaw Country Park

6 *Turn left immediately beyond the café, through a kissing gate and climb up to the road.*

7 *Turn left on the road and, after a few yards, turn right over a low stone stile. Climb the steep woodland path, following the rocky course of the stream.*

8 *Several paths meander over the bracken and gorse-covered hillside. Walk uphill, half left away from the stream, eventually joining a worn flagged path.*

Nether Padley

A View of Padley Gorge. This wild forested ravine is a reminder of what our native countryside once looked like.

B The mill, which is now a private house, relied upon Burbage Brook to power its wheels.

C Viewpoint. Look back across the intervening woodland towards the Derwent Valley with Eyam Moor in the distance.

D Viewpoint. The Upper Derwent stretches into the distance. Kinder Scout, Win Hill and Bleaklow form the final backcloth.

E Viewpoint. In May or June, pink and crimson flowers of the rhododendron bushes make an attractive foreground to the view.

F Longshaw Lodge. This Victorian hunting lodge and the surrounding estate is now owned by the National Trust.

G The low wall is a 'ha-ha'. Normally a 'ha-ha' is topped by a formal lawn which prevents animals from entering the garden, leaving the view from the house unspoiled.

Walk 16
BIRCHEN EDGE
4 miles (6.4km) Moderate

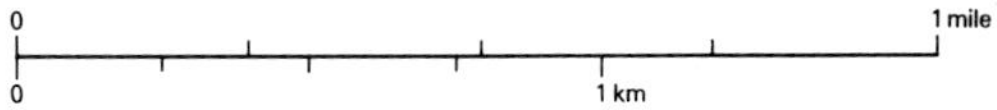

0 ——————————————— 1 mile
0 ————————— 1 km

Two monoliths, erected in memory of Nelson and Wellington, make excellent route markers for this walk. The route crosses stark gritstone edges on the skyline above Bar Brook, which offer magnificent views of the surrounding moors and parkland.

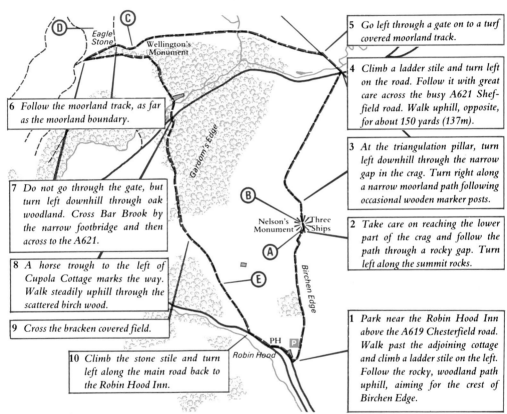

5 Go left through a gate on to a turf covered moorland track.

4 Climb a ladder stile and turn left on the road. Follow it with great care across the busy A621 Sheffield road. Walk uphill, opposite, for about 150 yards (137m).

6 Follow the moorland track, as far as the moorland boundary.

3 At the triangulation pillar, turn left downhill through the narrow gap in the crag. Turn right along a narrow moorland path following occasional wooden marker posts.

7 Do not go through the gate, but turn left downhill through oak woodland. Cross Bar Brook by the narrow footbridge and then across to the A621.

2 Take care on reaching the lower part of the crag and follow the path through a rocky gap. Turn left along the summit rocks.

8 A horse trough to the left of Cupola Cottage marks the way. Walk steadily uphill through the scattered birch wood.

9 Cross the bracken covered field.

1 Park near the Robin Hood Inn above the A619 Chesterfield road. Walk past the adjoining cottage and climb a ladder stile on the left. Follow the rocky, woodland path uphill, aiming for the crest of Birchen Edge.

10 Climb the stone stile and turn left along the main road back to the Robin Hood Inn.

Map labels: Eagle Stone, Wellington's Monument, Gardom's Edge, Nelson's Monument, Three Ships, Birchen Edge, Robin Hood, PH, P

A Nelson's Monument. Nearby are three boulders, each shaped like the bow of a man-of-war. They are fancifully named *Victory*, *Defiance* and *Soverin*; all ships at the Battle of Trafalgar.

B Viewpoint. Chatsworth House and its park fills the valley. To the left is the largest expanse of grouse moor in the Southern Pennines.

C Wellington Monument. The stone cross was erected in 1866. From here, there is a good view of Chatsworth House.

D The Eagle Stone is slightly off route but can be reached by a narrow sidepath. At one time, every young man from Baslow had to climb it before he could get married.

E A bracken covered mound, about halfway across the last field before the road, is the site of a prehistoric enclosure.

MILLER'S DALE AND WORMHILL
5 miles (8km) Moderate

Airy upland pastures on the limestone plateau contrast with the silvan beauty of two unspoiled dales on this walk. Monk's Dale is dry. Its river is beneath the limestone pavement but Miller's Dale has a base of impervious clay which holds the water of Derbyshire's River Wye, haunt of trout and river birds.

Wormhill is a little over half way round this walk. It is the birthplace of James Brindley, builder of much of England's canal system. The quiet village makes an ideal stopping place either to explore or perhaps to buy a pot of tea.

Miller's Dale station, once a busy junction where travellers to and from Buxton joined the main line to London, is now a useful car park and forms the northern end of the Monsal Trail.

A The twin viaducts once carried powerful steam locomotives hauling trains on a difficult section of the Midland Line along Monsal Dale. This line, from London St Pancras to Manchester Central, was originally planned to follow an easier route along the Derwent valley through Chatsworth Park to Hathersage. There it was to have joined the Sheffield/Manchester line. By 1849, when the line reached Rowsley near Matlock, the Duke of Devonshire sensed the threat to his beloved Chatsworth and refused the railway company the right of way across his property. Having failed to reach agreement with the duke, the railway company was forced to follow a more difficult route which climbed through Bakewell and then along the steep craggy sides of Monsal Dale. Even this plan was almost spoilt by the Duke of Rutland, who had to be placated by constructing an unnecessary tunnel beneath Haddon Hall and erecting a special station at Bakewell for his use. The saga of ducal autocracy only ended with the erection of a palatial station at rural Hassop, purely for the use of the Duke of Devonshire!

When the railway was first opened, the poet, Ruskin, suggested that it was just another means of exchanging one set of 'fools' for another as locals travelled between Buxton and Bakewell at the expense of the valley.

The Midland Line closed in the 1960s and is now used as the Monsal Trail. This walking trail is from Bakewell to Miller's Dale; tunnels are blocked and bypassed by either existing or concessionary paths but the Miller's Dale and Monsal Head viaducts, so hated by Ruskin, remain open for pedestrian use.

B Monksdale Farm. In the 14th century, there was a small chapel on the site of the farm — hence the name 'Monk's Dale'.

C Viewpoint. Look across the deep trough of Monk's Dale and Miller's Dale to Priestcliffe and the limestone uplands of Taddington Moor.

D Monk's Dale Viewpoint. The special flora and fauna of this densely wooded, narrow rocky dale are protected as part of a nature reserve. Peter Dale to the right, a continuation of Monk's Dale, is not as heavily wooded and more easily accessible.

E Viewpoint. Monk's Dale is to the east, continuing northwards towards Peak Forest as a series of inter-connecting dry dales.

F Wormhill. The quiet upland community will have changed very little since James Brindley, the canal engineer, was born here in 1716. Notice the ancient stocks to one side of the Brindley Memorial and spare a little time to look in on the 700-year-old village church.

G Viewpoint: the rocky buttress of Chee Tor is opposite.

H Viewpoint. Narrow terraces above Blackwell Dale, to the right of the main dale, mark the site of ancient fields. On the left-hand hillside are the remains of an old limestone quarry. The kilns have been preserved as an interesting archaeological feature and can be approached by a track beyond the Miller's Dale viaduct.

Over

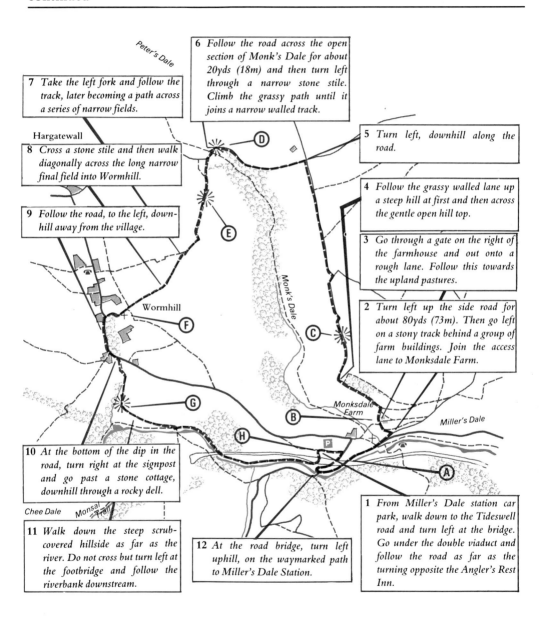

6 Follow the road across the open section of Monk's Dale for about 20yds (18m) and then turn left through a narrow stone stile. Climb the grassy path until it joins a narrow walled track.

7 Take the left fork and follow the track, later becoming a path across a series of narrow fields.

5 Turn left, downhill along the road.

8 Cross a stone stile and then walk diagonally across the long narrow final field into Wormhill.

4 Follow the grassy walled lane up a steep hill at first and then across the gentle open hill top.

9 Follow the road, to the left, downhill away from the village.

3 Go through a gate on the right of the farmhouse and out onto a rough lane. Follow this towards the upland pastures.

2 Turn left up the side road for about 80yds (73m). Then go left on a stony track behind a group of farm buildings. Join the access lane to Monksdale Farm.

10 At the bottom of the dip in the road, turn right at the signpost and go past a stone cottage, downhill through a rocky dell.

11 Walk down the steep scrub-covered hillside as far as the river. Do not cross but turn left at the footbridge and follow the riverbank downstream.

12 At the road bridge, turn left uphill, on the waymarked path to Miller's Dale Station.

1 From Miller's Dale station car park, walk down to the Tideswell road and turn left at the bridge. Go under the double viaduct and follow the road as far as the turning opposite the Angler's Rest Inn.

Peter's Dale

Hargatewall

Wormhill

Monk's Dale

Monksdale Farm

Miller's Dale

Chee Dale   Monsal Trail

Walk 18
TIDESWELL, MILLER'S AND CRESSBROOK DALES
7½ miles (12km) Moderate; one 400ft (122m) climb

Many people believe these to be the finest dales in the Peak. The quiet waters of the Wye flow through aptly-named Water cum Jolly, contrasting well with the mysterious ravine of Cressbrook Dale. Tideswell Dale provides further interest with its colourful wild flowers every summer.

A Viewpoint. An old quarry is above and to the left. It was exploited for brown dolerite, a form of basalt left by prehistoric volcanic activity. The steep limestone ramparts of Raven's Tor are ahead.

B Litton Mill. This old textile mill has a notorious history. It was founded in 1782, and was run on the virtual slave labour of orphans and other unfortunates who fell into the 'care' of the 'Guardians of the Poor'. Housed in crowded barracks which can still be seen beyond the mill, they worked a 15 hour, six day week, and were fed on gruel and thin broth augmented by oatcakes and black treacle.

C Viewpoint. The partly flooded section of the dale and its smooth walled limestone crags topped by steep grassy upper slopes, is known by the delightful name of Water cum Jolly Dale.

D Cressbrook Mill. This building is of considerable architectural merit but has ceased to produce textiles. Once powered by water, it was built originally for Richard Arkwright, father of the mechanised factory system.

E Viewpoint. Watercress still grows in Cressbrook's stream and the wooded dale is now a nature reserve. Ravenscliff Cave, in the crags on the eastern rim, was the home of some of our prehistoric forebears.

F Peter's Stone. This curious detached crag is reputed to be haunted by the last man to hang on a gibbet on its summit.

G Litton Village. Limestone cottages front a series of little greens and an ancient cross stands on one of them. They dress the Litton wells towards the end of June.

Over

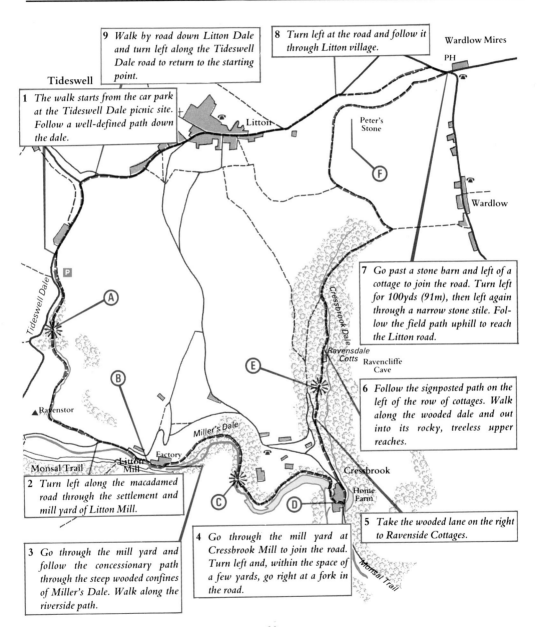

9 Walk by road down Litton Dale and turn left along the Tideswell Dale road to return to the starting point.

8 Turn left at the road and follow it through Litton village.

1 The walk starts from the car park at the Tideswell Dale picnic site. Follow a well-defined path down the dale.

7 Go past a stone barn and left of a cottage to join the road. Turn left for 100yds (91m), then left again through a narrow stone stile. Follow the field path uphill to reach the Litton road.

6 Follow the signposted path on the left of the row of cottages. Walk along the wooded dale and out into its rocky, treeless upper reaches.

2 Turn left along the macadamed road through the settlement and mill yard of Litton Mill.

5 Take the wooded lane on the right to Ravenside Cottages.

3 Go through the mill yard and follow the concessionary path through the steep wooded confines of Miller's Dale. Walk along the riverside path.

4 Go through the mill yard at Cressbrook Mill to join the road. Turn left and, within the space of a few yards, go right at a fork in the road.

Walk 19
SOLOMON'S TEMPLE
4½ miles (7.2km) Easy; uphill sections

Buxton has retained many of the attractions from its heyday as a spa town when visitors combined 'taking the waters' with an inland holiday. Re-opened after being abandoned for years, Pooles Cavern and its Visitor Centre give an interesting insight into the archaeological past.

The walk skirts Grin Low Woods and then climbs out on to the stark limestone moors before moving to Solomon's Temple with its vantage point above the town.

1 Walk along the road back towards the town and away from the Buxton Country Park/Poole's Cavern car park.

2 Turn right at a gap between the houses and walk through a series of fields.

3 Turn right along the macadam surfaced drive.

4 At a group of houses, cross a cattle grid and turn right. Climb the field boundary by the step stile and turn left. Follow the stone wall uphill and keep to the right of Fern House and its woodland. Continue ahead over the crest of the hill.

5 Bear left across the road and into the dip. Turn right through a gate on to a farm track.

6 Go through the farmyard and out along its access track, towards open fields of the limestone moor.

7 Turn right and follow the road for about ¼ mile (402m).

8 Turn left at a signpost, uphill along a cart track. Pass a group of untidy farm buildings, and follow the direction of a second signpost. Aim for the prominent tower on top of Grin Low.

9 Go downhill, through a narrow stile and then on to a second boundary wall. Do not cross the latter.

10 Turn left at the wall. Walk ahead on a cart track and enter the woods of Grin Plantation by climbing a gateside stile. Follow a wide path which gradually descends beneath the mature trees. Ignore any side paths.

11 Turn right down a flight of steps leading directly to the car park.

A Poole's Cavern. Classed as the 'First wonder of the Peak' by Charles Cotton in 1680, the natural cave was once the home of Stone Age Man. Open from Easter to early November, its history is explained in the adjacent Visitor Centre. Derbyshire's River Wye starts from this cave.

B Do not worry if you hear explosions coming from the strange cluster of buildings opposite. This is the Explosion and Fire Laboratory of the Health and Safety Executive where hazardous mixtures are tested under controlled conditions.

C Solomon's Temple. The tower was built in 1895 for a local worthy called Solomon Mycock, as a Victorian kind of job creation scheme. It sits on top of a prehistoric mound and at 1300ft (396m) it makes an excellent vantage point above Buxton and the surrounding moors.

SHINING TOR AND ERRWOOD

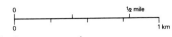

0   ½ mile

0   1 km

6½ miles (10.5km) Moderate; total ascent 896ft (273m); boggy sections

The scenery has changed from that of a hundred years ago. Two reservoirs now flood the deep wooded valley and a secluded stately home, once surrounded by formal grounds, is a sad ruin.

4 Turn left and follow the road uphill.

5 Leave the road by a signpost on the left and follow the moorland path uphill across Cats Tor to Shining Tor. Follow the boundary wall all the way.

6 Keep left at Shining Tor summit and cross the boggy upper head waters of Shooter's Clough. Keep to the left of the boundary wall.

7 Cross the wire boundary fence by the ladderstile. Then, almost immediately, go through a gap in the ruined wall to reach a wide track. Turn left along this old carriageway towards Errwood.

8 Bear right at the junction and follow the signposted path downhill back to the trail car park.

3 Cross a tiny footbridge and climb to the left, above the stream. Climb over the moor towards the road.

2 Cross the stream and climb along the old drive past the ruins of Errwood Hall. Beyond the hall, walk down to a second stream.

1 Follow the path uphill from the Nature Trail car park, through mixed woodland and rhododendron bushes, above the western arm of Errwood Reservoir.

Pym Chair — C

Oldgate Nick

Cats Tor

'The Shrine' — B

Foxlow Edge

The Tors

Shooter's Clough Bridge

Errwood Reservoir

Errwood Hall — A

Shining Tor — D

A Errwood Hall, once the home of the Grimshaw family, was built in 1830 and was the centre of a bustling community which existed until the late 1920s.

B The tiny circular building to the left of the path is a shrine built in memory of Dolores de Bergrin, the Spanish governess of the Grimshaw children.

C Viewpoint. On a clear day, the Cheshire Plain can be seen to the west; Alderley Edge is a final outlier of the Pennines and, beyond it, the Welsh Hills form the background. East, across the cleft of the Goyt Valley, is the wild moor of Combs Moss.

D Viewpoint. Macclesfield Forest, part of the Cheshire uplands, is dominated by the shapely peak of Shutlingsloe.

35

0   1 mile

0   1 km

4 miles (6.4km) Easy; one 420ft (128m) climb

People living in towns and cities surrounding the Peak District can reach its countryside in a very short period of time but none as quickly as those who live in the little industrial town of Bollington. This walk, which is a popular summer stroll for Bollington's inhabitants, starts beside the parish church and, after a short initial climb, it reaches the curious pear-shaped edifice on Kerridge Hill known as the White Nancy. The true history of the White Nancy seems to have been lost in the passage of time. We do not know who suggested its name or how its shape was decided upon. What is certain is that the local people of Bollington are very proud of this curious memorial and make sure that it is kept in good repair and given a coat of whitewash from time to time.

The height is gained, it must be admitted, by some effort but, once gained, it is retained for a mile (1.6km) or so, before you return along a pleasant side valley. This is a walk for lazy summer afternoons, or for an hour or so in the evening.

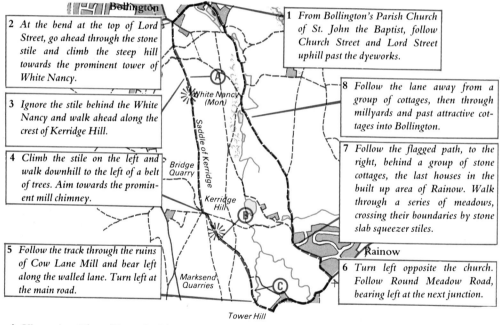

2 At the bend at the top of Lord Street, go ahead through the stone stile and climb the steep hill towards the prominent tower of White Nancy.

3 Ignore the stile behind the White Nancy and walk ahead along the crest of Kerridge Hill.

4 Climb the stile on the left and walk downhill to the left of a belt of trees. Aim towards the prominent mill chimney.

5 Follow the track through the ruins of Cow Lane Mill and bear left along the walled lane. Turn left at the main road.

1 From Bollington's Parish Church of St. John the Baptist, follow Church Street and Lord Street uphill past the dyeworks.

8 Follow the lane away from a group of cottages, then through millyards and past attractive cottages into Bollington.

7 Follow the flagged path, to the right, behind a group of stone cottages, the last houses in the built up area of Rainow. Walk through a series of meadows, crossing their boundaries by stone slab squeezer stiles.

6 Turn left opposite the church. Follow Round Meadow Road, bearing left at the next junction.

A Viewpoint. The whitewashed stone tower known as White Nancy is thought to commemorate the ending of the Napoleonic Wars. It looks to the west across the Cheshire Plain with the wooded sandstone ridge of Alderley Edge closer to hand. Eastwards, the outlook is towards Shining Tor and the Cat & Fiddle, England's second highest inn, which marks the moorland crossing of the A537.

B Viewpoint. The village of Rainow is below with the land rising towards the Cheshire Uplands. In the 18th century, the village 'mayor' was made to ride a donkey facing backwards during his inauguration ceremony.

C Cow Lane Mill. The ruins of a former textile mill.

Walk 22
MACCLESFIELD FOREST AND SHUTLINGSLOE
7 miles (11.3km) Strenuous; one 759ft (231m) climb

Shutlingsloe is not the highest point of normally flat Cheshire but it certainly has the best shape of any hill on this the western boundary of the Peak District. We cross its rocky summit on this walk through the Cheshire Uplands.

10 *Turn right at the pub, then right along the minor road, following it all the way back to Trentabank Reservoir. Keep right at all road junctions.*

1 *From the lay-by car park, climb the short flight of steps and then cross a stile. Walk uphill along the broad path through mature pine forest.*

Macclesfield Forest Chapel

Bottom-of-the-Oven

9 *Bear right across rough moorland pasture and then left, downhill on a sunken track, aiming directly towards the Hanging Gate Inn.*

Macclesfield Forest

Trentabank Reservoir

2 *Cross the stile in the upper forest boundary. Follow the signposted path out on to the open moor.*

8 *Keep below and left of both Oakenclough House and Farm. Cross the stream and climb to the access drive. Cross this and turn left uphill along an enclosed footpath.*

High Moor

Oakenclough

3 *Climb the stile and bear right over a stretch of boggy moor. Aim for the prominent summit of Shutlingsloe.*

Shutlingsloe Farm

Crag Hall

7 *Cross a stile on the right by the side of Greenway Bridge. Follow waymarks upstream towards Oakenclough. Keep left at the junction with a lesser stream and then right of a small ruined barn.*

Piggford Moor

Greenway Bridge

Wildboarclough

4 *Follow yellow arrows, steeply downhill through the summit rocks and across the lower moor. Cross the boundary wall by its stile and, still following waymarks, keep well to the right of the farm buildings. Turn right on the access drive and join the valley road conveniently close to the Crag Inn.*

6 *Climb the stile and join the farm lane near a sharp bend. Turn left and follow the lane as far as the road, then turn right.*

5 *Climb the flight of steps in the roadside wall at the corner of the pub car park. Follow the grassy path above a clump of thorn bushes. Cross a series of pathless fields as indicated by waymarks and stiles.*

A Trentabank Reservoir Nature Reserve. A plaque shows the commonest visiting and resident waterfowl on this attractive reservoir within Macclesfield Forest.

B Shutlingsloe, 1659ft (506m). A commemorative plaque in the summit rocks gives the names of the prominent features seen from this vantage point. The valley, which the route next follows, is Wildboarclough and the ornamental lake opposite is within the grounds of Crag Hall, part of the estate of Lord Derby.

C Viewpoint. Shutlingsloe is opposite, above Piggford Moor.

D Viewpoint. Tegg's Nose Country Park includes the overgrown quarries on the skyline. Below, the mature pines of Macclesfield Forest fill the valley and the scene is completed by Langley's twin reservoirs.

Walk 23
DOVEDALE

4½ miles (7.2km) Moderate; one 538ft (164m) climb

Most visitors arriving at the lower reaches of Dovedale are content with a short stroll beyond the stepping stones at the mouth of the dale. Scenically delightful though this may be, it is only a mere hint of the attractions further upstream.

Old prints and photographs show the dale sides almost bare of trees but, in the space of a few decades, the valley became over populated by the rapid spread of ash and sycamore. In the old days, sheep and cattle were grazed within the confines of the dale which prevented the growth of intrusive saplings. Now that they no longer graze there, as a result of more intensive modern farming methods, the dale has lost this natural method of restricting the invasive spread of dense woodland. The National Trust, as owners of Dovedale, have lately been removing much of this new growth from around special features. As a result, natural formations such as Reynard's Cave and the Twelve Apostles' Rocks, can be appreciated as they were in the past. Grass is now regenerating, holding the loose scree and the view of Dovedale is now more open. Overused footpaths have been repaired and erosion stopped. This remedial work, together with the drastic tree removal has not been to everyone's taste but the dale was changing and scenic features were disappearing beneath the crowding trees. Something had to be done and now that nature, assisted by the National Trust, has taken over again, Dovedale's beauty is being preserved for the future.

A St. Bertram's Well. St. Bertram or Bertelin brought Christianity to Dovedale in the seventh or eighth century. Legend tells us that he became a hermit following the death of his Irish born wife and his only child who were attacked by a pack of wolves nearby. Heartbroken, he spent the rest of his life in this remote hollow.

B Viewpoint. The mock tudor chimneys of Victorian Ilam Hall can be seen in the valley bottom. Beyond the hall, Hinckley Wood shrouds the steep sides of the lower Manifold Valley.

C Viewpoint. Air Cottage must have one of the finest views in the Peak District. Set high above Dovedale, you can see Thorpe Cloud on the right, then Lover's Leap, Tissington Spires and Reynard's Cave. The middle and upper dale can be seen curving away to the north as a narrow ravine cleaving its way through the limestone uplands.

D Lion Rock at the foot of Pickering Tor is aptly named. Look back upstream for the best view.

E Reynard's Cave. Look out for a natural arch high above the path on the left. A cave beyond the arch was used as a hiding place during troubled times following the end of the Roman occupation. Arrow heads and pottery have been found in its recesses.

F Lover's Leap. The path climbs above the river by a series of steps to reach this rocky vantage point. Opposite, there are rocky spires known as the Twelve Apostles. Autumn is the best time for this part of the dale because this is when the trees are most colourful. There is no record of any star-crossed lovers jumping from this point but there is a cautionary tale concerning the Irish Dean of Clogher. In 1761 he tried to ride over the rock carrying a young lady companion as a pillion passenger. The horse stumbled on the slippery rocks and all three fell towards the river. The Dean was killed and is buried at Ashbourne. The lady was more fortunate, however, as she was saved by her long hair which caught in the branches of a tree.

Over

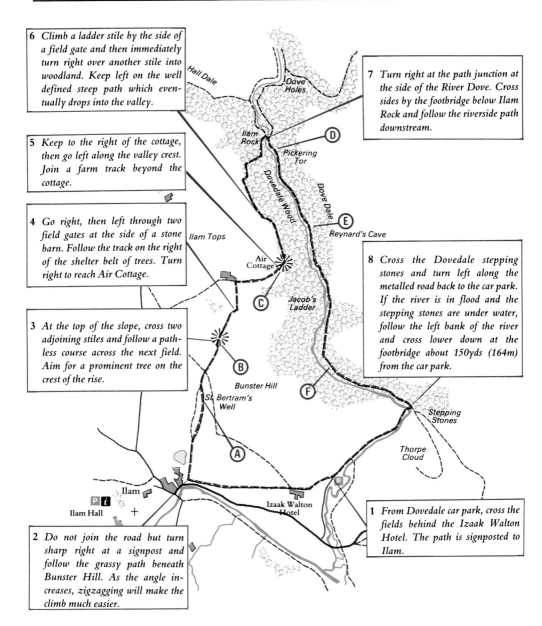

6 Climb a ladder stile by the side of a field gate and then immediately turn right over another stile into woodland. Keep left on the well defined steep path which eventually drops into the valley.

7 Turn right at the path junction at the side of the River Dove. Cross sides by the footbridge below Ilam Rock and follow the riverside path downstream.

5 Keep to the right of the cottage, then go left along the valley crest. Join a farm track beyond the cottage.

4 Go right, then left through two field gates at the side of a stone barn. Follow the track on the right of the shelter belt of trees. Turn right to reach Air Cottage.

8 Cross the Dovedale stepping stones and turn left along the metalled road back to the car park. If the river is in flood and the stepping stones are under water, follow the left bank of the river and cross lower down at the footbridge about 150yds (164m) from the car park.

3 At the top of the slope, cross two adjoining stiles and follow a pathless course across the next field. Aim for a prominent tree on the crest of the rise.

2 Do not join the road but turn sharp right at a signpost and follow the grassy path beneath Bunster Hill. As the angle increases, zigzagging will make the climb much easier.

1 From Dovedale car park, cross the fields behind the Izaak Walton Hotel. The path is signposted to Ilam.

39

Walk 24
THE ROACHES
7 miles (11.3km) Moderate/Strenuous; one 608ft (185m) climb

The Roaches provide some of the finest and longest gritstone climbs in the Peak District. This is where many of the famous local climbers such as Joe Brown and the late Don Whillans first developed their skills. Routes of every standard can be found on these crags and climbers will be seen almost every day of the year attempting what might seem impossibly acrobatic moves.

French monks established their Dieulacresse Abbey close by; below what is now Tittesworth Reservoir. They, with what in hindsight sounds like a lack of imagination, gave the crags the name 'Rocher' which is French for 'rock'. The name changed to Roaches at a later date but lingers in the old form at Roche Grange.

Today the moors and the Roaches themselves are owned by the Peak Park Planning Board. In buying the Roaches Estate, the Board have opened up access to the rocks for climbers and also established a number of concessionary footpaths over the moors, several of which are used to advantage on this walk.

About half way along the walk, the route passes through Lud Church, a roofless fern bedecked cave caused by a landslip in the gritstone strata. This strange gorge is linked with legends and it can be a spooky place on the sunniest of days.

Do not be alarmed if you see wallabies on this walk. It will have nothing to do with any pre-walk visit to the nearby Rock Inn! There really are wallabies on the moors around the Roaches. These marsupials are the descendants of animals released during World War II from a private zoo established by Lt. Col. Brocklehurst who had been a game warden in the Sudan. At one time there was even a yak wandering about on the moors, much to the consternation of unsuspecting walkers and climbers!

A small number of wallabies have managed to survive despite the harsh winters. Please respect these shy creatures and do not try to find them. Keep dogs under control at all times and you may be rewarded by an unexpected glimpse of these strange creatures.

A Rockhall Cottage. As this building is inhabited, please do not attempt to climb the perimeter wall.

B Viewpoint. The dramatic peak of Hen Cloud is to the southeast. Beyond, the North Staffordshire Plain stretches into the distance.

C Doxey Pool. This little pool does not appear to have either an inlet or outlet.

D Viewpoint. Shutlingsloe, Cheshire's 'Matterhorn', rises above the Dane Valley and the hills of North Wales can often be seen in hazy outline across the Cheshire Plain. Approximately due west, The Cloud can be seen.

E Lud's Church. It is said that the cave was a refuge for Walter de Ludank, a follower of Wycliffe who held dissenting services here in the 14th century. A more ancient legend connects it with the Green Chapel of the medieval poem 'Sir Gawain and the Green Knight'. If this is correct, then it was on this spot that King Arthur's champion met and fought the green knight.

F Viewpoint. Castle Cliff Rocks make an ideal picnic spot above the Upper Dane.

G Viewpoint. The nearby valley is the Dane.

H At one time there were many small farms in this area. Their owners eked out a bare living by mining coal in shallow pits on the moors. Many of the small holdings still exist, with the present day owners working in nearby towns and farming in their spare time.

Over

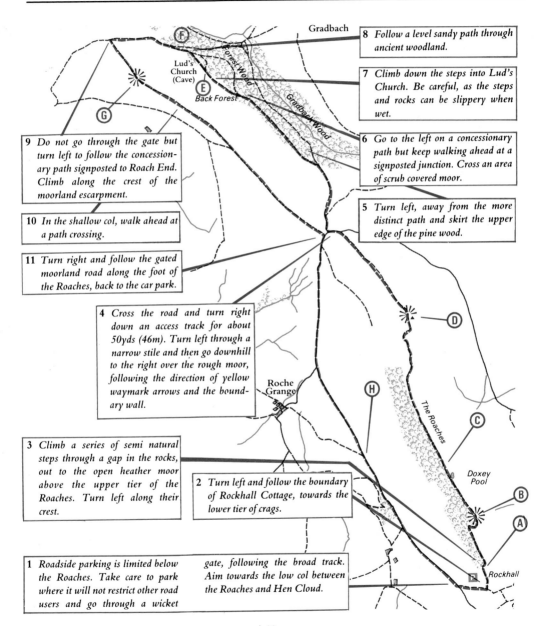

8 Follow a level sandy path through ancient woodland.

7 Climb down the steps into Lud's Church. Be careful, as the steps and rocks can be slippery when wet.

6 Go to the left on a concessionary path but keep walking ahead at a signposted junction. Cross an area of scrub covered moor.

5 Turn left, away from the more distinct path and skirt the upper edge of the pine wood.

9 Do not go through the gate but turn left to follow the concessionary path signposted to Roach End. Climb along the crest of the moorland escarpment.

10 In the shallow col, walk ahead at a path crossing.

11 Turn right and follow the gated moorland road along the foot of the Roaches, back to the car park.

4 Cross the road and turn right down an access track for about 50yds (46m). Turn left through a narrow stile and then go downhill to the right over the rough moor, following the direction of yellow waymark arrows and the boundary wall.

3 Climb a series of semi natural steps through a gap in the rocks, out to the open heather moor above the upper tier of the Roaches. Turn left along their crest.

2 Turn left and follow the boundary of Rockhall Cottage, towards the lower tier of crags.

1 Roadside parking is limited below the Roaches. Take care to park where it will not restrict other road users and go through a wicket gate, following the broad track. Aim towards the low col between the Roaches and Hen Cloud.

Gradbach

Lud's Church (Cave)

Forest Wood

Back Forest

Gradbach Wood

Roche Grange

The Roaches

Doxey Pool

Rockhall

CHELMORTON AND DEEPDALE
4¼ miles (6.8km) Moderate; rocky in Deep Dale

People have been living around Chelmorton for thousands of years. Their early burial mounds are on the surrounding heights and, nearby, is the mysterious stone tomb of Five Wells. Badly damaged by early archaeologists, there were once two chambers within this limestone cairn containing pottery and flint tools.

Chelmorton is a linear village with its houses filling the gaps between farms. They all use the water source which flows from a well above the church at the head of the village. The church of St. John the Baptist has its traditional locust weather vane and is at least 700 years old.

Chelmorton sits at the bottom of a west-facing slope, covered by a unique pattern of narrow walled fields — the preserved relics of medieval husbandry. Oxen were used to drag ploughs in the middle ages and these lumbering beasts and the early ploughs were difficult to turn. As a result, fields tended to be long and narrow, with each farmer working those around his farm and sharing common grazing on larger fields beyond the village.

Deep Dale is a complete contrast to the ancient fields above its ravine. With the exception of the stark ugliness of Topley Pike Quarry, the dale is completely unspoiled and nature is in command. Away from the quarry, the path is across rough stony ground and care must taken, otherwise a twisted ankle could mar a fascinating walk.

A Chelmorton's complex field system is laid out across the gentle slope behind the village. No longer suitable for efficient farming methods, the walls and the field patterns are preserved with co-operation from the farmers and grants from the Peak District National Park.

B Viewpoint. The northern dales, which drain into the Derbyshire River Wye, reach out from the gritstone moors of the Dark Peak. In the middle distance you can see some of the major limestone quarries of the Peak which provide work for the local population.

C Humps in the surrounding grazing denote the boundaries of a Celtic field system, even older than the fields marked by the stone walls around Chelmorton.

D Churn Holes. To the right, where the path zigzags steeply through a gap in the limestone crag, there is a series of shallow holes created by water action at the end of the Ice Age.

E Topley Pike suddenly hits the senses. It is a hard fact of life that limestone, needed for safe roads, is mostly found in beautiful areas such as the Peak District.

F Deep Dale. Beyond the slurry lagoon, the tranquillity of Deep Dale soon takes over. Specialised plants and shrubby trees live on the sparse rock-strewn soil. The dale bottom is damp but, above it, dry scree slopes lead to limestone crags. Caves in the crags on both sides of the dale below Raven's Tor, were once the dwellings of stone age man.

G The path along Horseshoe Dale is known as the Priest's Way and probably dates from the time when much of the land in the Peak was owned by various monasteries. The track could have been used to connect the grange or 'granary' near Brierlow with pasture above King's Sterndale.

H The roughly worked opening at the bottom of Bullhay Dale, on the left of the path, is an adit, or mine entrance. This one time lead mine was worked for its fluorspar in recent years. A useless hindrance to lead miners, fluorspar is used as a flux in the manufacture of steel and as a source of the gas, fluorine. What was once a waste product is now a valuable commodity in the Peak.

Do not, on any account, go inside the mine as it is in a dangerous condition.

Over

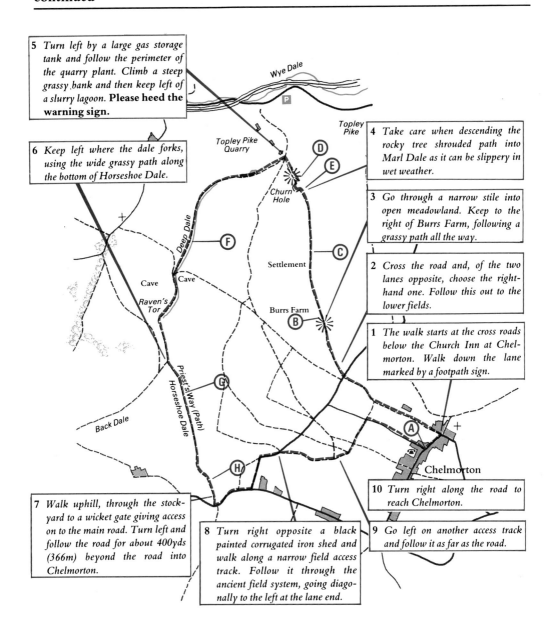

5 Turn left by a large gas storage tank and follow the perimeter of the quarry plant. Climb a steep grassy bank and then keep left of a slurry lagoon. **Please heed the warning sign.**

6 Keep left where the dale forks, using the wide grassy path along the bottom of Horseshoe Dale.

4 Take care when descending the rocky tree shrouded path into Marl Dale as it can be slippery in wet weather.

3 Go through a narrow stile into open meadowland. Keep to the right of Burrs Farm, following a grassy path all the way.

2 Cross the road and, of the two lanes opposite, choose the right-hand one. Follow this out to the lower fields.

1 The walk starts at the cross roads below the Church Inn at Chelmorton. Walk down the lane marked by a footpath sign.

10 Turn right along the road to reach Chelmorton.

7 Walk uphill, through the stockyard to a wicket gate giving access on to the main road. Turn left and follow the road for about 400yds (366m) beyond the road into Chelmorton.

8 Turn right opposite a black painted corrugated iron shed and walk along a narrow field access track. Follow it through the ancient field system, going diagonally to the left at the lane end.

9 Go left on another access track and follow it as far as the road.

Walk 26
CHATSWORTH
6 miles (9.6km) Moderate; one 600ft (183m) climb

Walkers are free to roam over much of the parkland and woods surrounding Chatsworth, and this walk takes advantage of that opportunity. Starting by first moving away from Chatsworth Park, the walk visits Beeley. Its houses are built of gritstone with a warm, grey hue and the church seems slightly aloof from the rest of the village. Every spring, its graveyard is a mass of wild daffodils.

Beyond Beeley, the route climbs inappropriately named Hell Bank Plantation to reach the open space of Beeley Moor. It then descends, only to climb again by a concessionary path into sheltering game forests to the east of Chatsworth House.

A Viewpoint. The view is downward across the pine forest of Hell Bank Plantation and then by way of Beeley to the Derwent Valley. The Wye Valley and limestone uplands are beyond.

B Swiss Cottage (private). This quaint Victorian folly lies across Swiss Lake. Pheasants bred in the surrounding forest often give themselves away by their raucous rattle. More gentle sounds come from the smaller woodland birds of the area.

C Emperor Lake. The lake provides the natural pressure to lift water 290ft (88m) high in the Emperor Fountain, one of Chatsworth's many features. This spectacular fountain can be seen over a considerable distance when fully operational. It was made to impress Tsar Nicholas I of Russia who, unfortunately, never came to see it.

D The Elizabethan Hunting Tower was built to enable the ladies of Chatsworth to watch the hunt in the parkland below. Chatsworth spreads in all its glory. The present house, home of the Dukes of Devonshire, was built in the 17th century in the Palladian style. Capability Brown landscaped the park and its gardens but the present gardens were designed by Sir Joseph Paxton (1803–1865) for the sixth Duke.

Edensor (pronounced 'Ensor') is beyond the small hill across the river from the Hall. Until 1838, the village stood closer to the Hall, but the sixth Duke decided to have the whole village moved as he felt it spoiled his view. Every house in the village, though built at the same time, is different. The story is that the Duke, on looking through an architect's catalogue, could not make up his mind and had one built in each design! This ducal 'compulsory purchase order' is incomplete, as one house from the old village remains. It is the old cottate opposite Edensor and is said to have been left there because the tennant, a Mr. Hughes, stood up to the duke and refused to be rehoused.

E The Queen Mary's Bower. The moated tower, a little to the right of the bridge is all that remains of the Elizabethan Chatsworth built by Bess of Hardwick.

Mary Queen of Scots, in her sad and long captivity, was imprisoned at Chatsworth in the care of the Earl of Shrewsbury, husband of Bess. The Bower is said to have been one of her favourite haunts. It was Bess's grandson who became the first Duke of Devonshire by helping William III to gain the throne. The title should be 'Derbyshire' but, due to a clerical error, it became 'Devonshire'.

F Viewpoint. This is the most famous view of the house. You can tell, by the number of young trees, that the park is constantly being updated. This is to preserve the scene laid out by Capability Brown two hundred years ago.

G The Old Mill. This was the estate mill, last used in 1950 for grinding corn. Severely damaged by a storm in 1962, the romantic ruin has been preserved as part of the park. Remnants of the water wheel and grinding machinery can still be seen inside the otherwise empty shell.

Over

44

0   1 mile

0   1 km

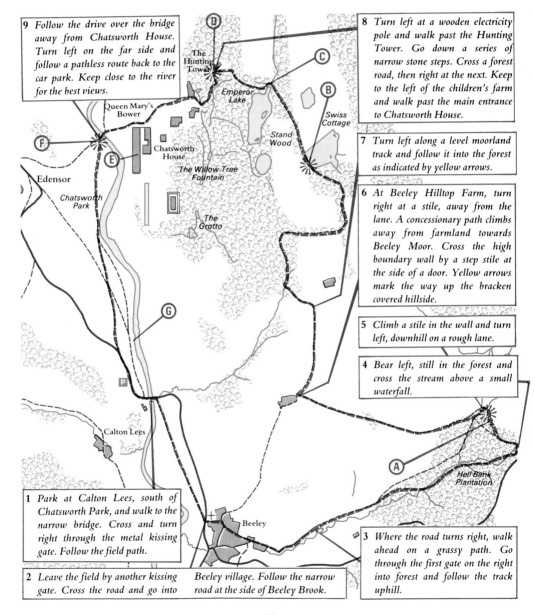

9 *Follow the drive over the bridge away from Chatsworth House. Turn left on the far side and follow a pathless route back to the car park. Keep close to the river for the best views.*

8 *Turn left at a wooden electricity pole and walk past the Hunting Tower. Go down a series of narrow stone steps. Cross a forest road, then right at the next. Keep to the left of the children's farm and walk past the main entrance to Chatsworth House.*

7 *Turn left along a level moorland track and follow it into the forest as indicated by yellow arrows.*

6 *At Beeley Hilltop Farm, turn right at a stile, away from the lane. A concessionary path climbs away from farmland towards Beeley Moor. Cross the high boundary wall by a step stile at the side of a door. Yellow arrows mark the way up the bracken covered hillside.*

5 *Climb a stile in the wall and turn left, downhill on a rough lane.*

4 *Bear left, still in the forest and cross the stream above a small waterfall.*

1 *Park at Calton Lees, south of Chatsworth Park, and walk to the narrow bridge. Cross and turn right through the metal kissing gate. Follow the field path.*

3 *Where the road turns right, walk ahead on a grassy path. Go through the first gate on the right into forest and follow the track uphill.*

2 *Leave the field by another kissing gate. Cross the road and go into* Beeley village. *Follow the narrow road at the side of Beeley Brook.*

The Hunting Tower
Emperor Lake
Queen Mary's Bower
Swiss Cottage
Stand Wood
Chatsworth House
The Willow Tree Fountain
Edensor
Chatsworth Park
The Grotto
Calton Lees
Beeley
Hell Bank Plantation

MONSAL DALE

6½ miles (10.5km) Easy/Moderate

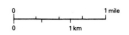

Gentle field paths lead to Monsal Head, where there is one of the finest views in the Peak. Beyond it, the route follows the tree lined River Wye back to an unspoiled village.

6 Walk through the car park and a narrow stile to the right of the café. Take the second path on the left and go downhill across the scrub covered hillside as far as the river.

5 Turn left along the road. Follow it past the cosy Pack Horse Inn as far as Monsal Head.

7 Cross the footbridge and then turn left, downstream along the river.

4 Climb on to the old railway track and turn left. Follow the yellow 'M' waymarks of the Monsal Trail to the right, away from the railway, over fields into Little Longstone.

8 Go carefully across the busy A6 to the picnic site. Follow a field path waymarked 2,3,8.

3 Cross the road to join the path along a shallow grassy valley.

9 Go left over the wooden stile, then forwards along the scrub shrouded path through the gap in a low limestone crag. Climb the open hillside.

2 Turn right down a walled track signposted to Little Longstone. Cross boundary walls by their stiles.

10 Turn half left, slanting uphill through Demon's Dell.

13 Turn left across Sheepwash Bridge to re-enter Ashford-in-the-Water.

1 From Ashford-in-the-Water, turn left opposite the Devonshire Arms and walk up Greaves Lane (Monsal Head road), for about ¼ mile (402m).

11 Cross the stile and walk along a well made path through mature woodland.

12 Go left at the road and then right along the grass verge of the A6.

A Monsal Trail follows part of the Midland Line which ran through the Monsal Dale gorge. Linking paths avoid tunnels and abandoned bridges between Bakewell and Miller's Dale.

B Monsal Head viewpoint. The River Wye curves below, crossed spectacularly by a viaduct which was hated by Victorian environmentalist and poet, John Ruskin, but now makes a graceful addition to the landscape.

C Viewpoint. Great Shacklow Wood covers the righthand hillside above the A6. Fin Cop, topped by its ancient earthwork, is opposite.

D Water issuing from a channel beneath the path is from a sough draining nearby Magpie lead mine.

E Two partly repaired water mills on the left made bobbins and spindles for Richard Arkwright's mills in Bakewell and Cressbrook.

F The small overgrown quarry (Arrock Mine), on the right, produced black marble in Victorian times.

G Sheepwash Bridge is named after the sheep dip at its side. Beyond the bridge is the market stand and a nearby plaque tells a little of the history of Ashford.

Walk 28
MONYASH AND FLAGG
8 miles (12.9km) Easy

0   1 mile
0   1 km

Monyash developed around the local lead mines. At one time it had a Barmote Court to settle mining disputes and a weekly market which met by a stone cross in front of what is now the Hobbit Inn. Flagg, on the other hand, is a linear village, consisting mostly of farms which rely on the nearby spring for their supplies of water.

5 Cross a grassy strip to reach the road. Turn left through a gate by the 'T' junction. There is no path: follow a diagonal line across the field. Line up gates and stiles to cross a series of narrow fields as far as Rockfield House.

6 Keep to the right of the farm. Turn right at the road for about 100yds (91m), then left at a footpath sign. Follow the field path to Flagg, entering the village by way of Hall Farm's stock yard.

7 Follow the road away from the village.

8 Leave the road to walk along the farm lane.

9 Keep to the right of Knotlow Farm, aiming for two prominent ash trees at the top of the field.

4 Turn left at the track crossroads.

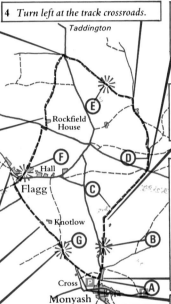

Taddington

Rockfield House

Sheldon

Hall

Flagg

Knotlow

Cross

Monyash

3 Cross the road and walk down the cart lane. Ignore waymarked path 8, diverging on the right, and continue uphill along the lane.

2 Go to the right of a shelter belt of trees. Continue to cross boundary walls by their stiles as indicated by the yellow arrows.

1 The Walk starts at the Jack Mere car park in Monyash. Walk northwards, away from the village, to a road junction and turn right for about 50 yds (46m). Cross over a stile on the left (signposted to Taddington) and then pass through a series of meadows.

10 Go past a stone barn to the right of an open grassy area and follow the walled lane.

11 Go left through a squeezer stile and cross the narrow fields by a series of stiles. Enter the village at the side of a row of cottages.

A Jack Mere, now filled in, was one of five artificial pools, or meres, which provided water for the village. Monyash or 'Many ash' appears in the Doomsday Book as 'Maneis'.

B Viewpoint. Look back at the village. The church steeple is the focal point but narrow strip fields, 'fossilised' in their medieval system, are all around.

C Strips of mature woodland in the Peak have a dual purpose. They provide a wind break on the exposed upland but their main purpose was to exclude cattle from areas poisoned by lead waste.

D Notice the heather growing on either side of the lane, a rarity in a normally alkaline region.

E Viewpoint of the upper Lathkill basin with Monyash in the distance and Flagg closer to hand.

F Viewpoint. Flagg, an example of a linear village which developed along a spring line — a rarity on dry limestone uplands.

G From here, there is a good view of Monyash across its 'home' fields.

YOULGREAVE AND LATHKILL DALE
8 miles (12.9km) Easy/Moderate

The walk begins in Youlgreave — a village which is linked, albeit historically, with lead mining. Some of the oldest village buildings are still farms and are firmly part of the village structure despite modern development.

Officially, Youlgreave is usually spelt with an 'e' but the locals prefer it as Youlgrave.

Below the village, in quiet Bradford Dale, trout pools originally provided water to power both corn and lead smelt mills. Climbing out of the dale, the walk follows a series of grassy paths across the lush pastures of Calling Low Farm. Gentle breezes blow on the farm, even on the sunniest of days but in winter the story is entirely different. Extensive shelterbelts of trees are planted to break the force of winter gales. Through the trees, one of the finest views across the limestone plateau opens up. Dropping quickly into Cales Dale, the path then leads through the sylvan tranquillity of Lathkill Dale, a dale which was once the scene of intensive mining activity but is now a completely natural valley.

A Opposite the youth hostel, there is a large circular stone water tank. On the dry limestone plateau, obtaining water has been a problem which Youlgreave has overcome by bringing it across Bradford Dale from nearby Stanton Moor. The village is one of the few places with a private water supply. An annual well dressing celebration marks Youlgreave's appreciation for the gift of pure water.

B Middleton-by-Youlgreave stands at the head of Bradford Dale. You can reach it from stage four of the route by turning left instead of right at the main road. One of several Peakland Middletons, this sleepy village was the home of Christopher Fullwood, who raised an army of 1000 lead miners during the Civil War. Thomas Bateman, the 19th century archaeologist, also lived here. Together with teams of local labourers, he dug out large numbers of ancient burial mounds, in a misguided search for treasure.

C The road crosses a tree lined cutting following the line of Long Rake lead vein. Latterly, the Rake has been worked from the surface to extract fluorspar.

D Viewpoint. Lathkill Dale is the wooded ravine to your right and Monyash church spire can be glimpsed in the distance. Directly opposite, across Cales Dale, is One Ash Grange, a prosperous sheep farm, once a monastic penitentiary.

E Natural woodland covering the opposite hillside is part of a nature reserve.

F Stone pillars mark the line of a viaduct which carried water across the dale to Mandale Mine.

G Mandale was one of the largest lead mines in the locality but only the shell of its pit-head gear now remains. **As with all old mines, it is best not to go too close.**

H A notice near the woodland edge lays claim to the private ownership of the path by stating that, on the Thursday of Easter week, anyone using it can be charged one penny.

I Over Haddon is to the left, about ½ mile (0.8km) away by the steep side road. There are several cafés and one pub.

J Youlgreave's historic church is well worth a visit. Look inside at the radiant colours of the east window. The Norman font, with an upside down dragon holding an oil stoup in its mouth, was originally the property of Elton Church. It was thrown out of Elton Church during reconstruction work in Victorian times and found its way to Youlgreave. Inter-village rivalry was only settled when Elton agreed to make do with a copy.

Over

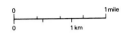

0   1 mile

0   1 km

12 *Enter private woodland by following a concessionary footpath.*

11 *Cross the wooden footbridge and turn right, following the riverside path along Lathkill Dale.*

13 *At the end of the wood, go right, then left around the boundary of a large house. Follow the path along the river bank.*

14 *On reaching the road, turn right over Conksbury Bridge for about 120yds (110m), then left through a squeezer stile on to a field path. Notices at this point will inform you that teas are on sale at Conksbury Farm 100yds (91m) further up the road.*

10 *Climb the stile and go steeply down the stepped path into shrubby Cales Dale. Turn right along the dale bottom.*

9 *Keep left, following signs through Calling Low farmyard.*

15 *Follow the field path. Turn right at a narrow lane, past Raper Lodge to reach Youlgreave.*

Over Haddon

Shaft (dis)

Lathkill Dale

One Ash Grange Farm

River Lathkill

Conksbury Bridge

Cales Dale

Calling Low

Raper Lodge

Youlgreave

8 *Climb the wall stile on the right and cross a series of grassy fields, following occasional waymark posts.*

7 *Turn left along the road and keep straight on at the junction.*

River Bradford

Middleton

1 *Car parking can usually be found at either end of the village. The walk starts in the main street.*

6 *Climb the stile on the right and follow a field path uphill as far as the Moor Lane picnic site.*

2 *Turn left down Holywell Lane past the village hall to reach Bradford Dale.*

5 *Follow the road to the second bend and go left through a stone squeezer stile at the side of a white gate. Cross the field and reach the upper road by a step stile. Ignore the path opposite but turn left to follow the road for about 50yds (46m).*

4 *Cross the stream by a broad stone bridge on the right, then go left uphill past a ruined mill. Walk beneath trees as far as the road, then turn right.*

3 *Cross a stone clapper bridge and turn right to follow the riverside path upstream past a series of trout pools.*

Walk 30
LONGNOR TWO VALLEYS WALK
4 miles (6.4km) Easy

From the village of Longnor, we visit two major Peakland valleys. At first, the underlying strata is shale and the River Manifold flows in a broad fertile trough but, across Sheen Moor, the River Dove has carved a steep sided valley through its limestone bedrock.

7 Go left along the wide grassy river access track. Cross the footbridge, then climb a low rise to reach a shallow side valley.

6 Leave the side road. Follow the signpost along a lane to open fields.

8 Turn left at a stone barn and climb along a gravel lane to Longnor.

1 Follow the road east from Longnor for about 150yds (137m). Turn right along the signposted lane to Folds End Farm. Go left through the farmyard. Climb over a stone stile and turn half right to follow a field path to the River Manifold.

2 Turn left along the gravel surfaced farm track. Keep left through the farmyard and then right on a rutted track. Follow it past a white gate and go through the next gate. Walk uphill on the field track as far as the road.

5 Cross the river by the footbridge. Follow the track beyond it as far as the lane and turn left into Crowdicote. Go right on the main road, then left along a side lane.

4 Climb the stile at the top of the farm garden. Follow a waymarked path. Cross a private lane. Follow yellow waymarks. Pass a barn and, following waymarks and stiles, cross a series of fields to the River Dove. Walk upstream.

3 Turn right along the road for about 500yds (457m). Climb the stone stile and turn left across three fields. Turn right, down the track to Under Whitle Farm.

Beggar's Bridge

Crowdecote

Longnor

Folds End

Ⓐ Ⓑ Ⓒ Ⓓ Ⓔ Ⓟ

Motte and Baileys

Pilsbury Castle Hills

A Longnor. There is no longer a market but a renovated plaque above the market hall has a list of the tolls due to the Harpur-Crewe estate.

B Viewpoint. Longnor village is above the Manifold valley. The grassy shoulder beyond Longnor marks the boundary between gritstone and shales of the Western Part and the Dovedale limestone.

C View of the Upper Dove. Grassy mounds in the valley bottom mark the motte and bailey of Pilsbury Castle.

D Crowdicote. The village is named after Saxon Cruda who built the first farm on this spot. The Pack Horse Inn is a welcome sight on a hot day.

E View of the upper Dove and the reef knoll hills of its eastern flank.

Walk 31
ELTON AND ROBIN HOOD'S STRIDE
3 miles (4.8km) Easy/Moderate

0   ½ mile
0   1 km

The walk starts in Elton where the friendly cottages were once the homes of lead miners. On the surrounding upland, the route passes several pre-Christian remains and a hermit's cave.

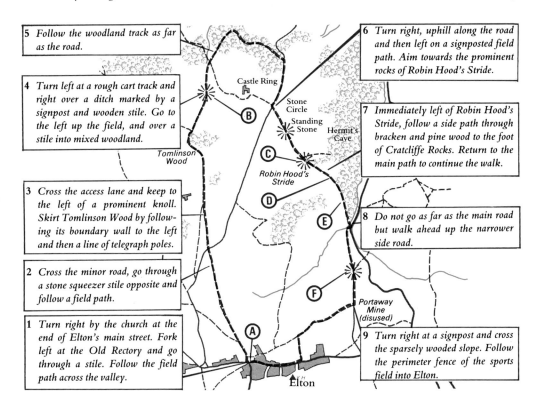

5 Follow the woodland track as far as the road.

4 Turn left at a rough cart track and right over a ditch marked by a signpost and wooden stile. Go to the left up the field, and over a stile into mixed woodland.

3 Cross the access lane and keep to the left of a prominent knoll. Skirt Tomlinson Wood by following its boundary wall to the left and then a line of telegraph poles.

2 Cross the minor road, go through a stone squeezer stile opposite and follow a field path.

1 Turn right by the church at the end of Elton's main street. Fork left at the Old Rectory and go through a stile. Follow the field path across the valley.

6 Turn right, uphill along the road and then left on a signposted field path. Aim towards the prominent rocks of Robin Hood's Stride.

7 Immediately left of Robin Hood's Stride, follow a side path through bracken and pine wood to the foot of Cratcliffe Rocks. Return to the main path to continue the walk.

8 Do not go as far as the main road but walk ahead up the narrower side road.

9 Turn right at a signpost and cross the sparsely wooded slope. Follow the perimeter fence of the sports field into Elton.

Castle Ring
Stone Circle
Ⓑ
Standing Stone
Hermit's Cave
Ⓒ
Tomlinson Wood
Robin Hood's Stride
Ⓓ
Ⓔ
Ⓕ
Portaway Mine (disused)
Ⓐ
Elton

A Elton is a village which once made its living from lead mining. In fact, there was a mine next to the church — you can see where it was from the rough ground next to the church yard. The font inside the church has an unusual history. When the church was rebuilt in Victorian times, the original font found its way to Youlgreave and Elton had to make do with a copy.

B Viewpoint. Youlgreave sits astride its ridge above Bradford Dale.

C Viewpoint. Robin Hood's Stride dominates the skyline in front. To the left in the corner of a field, stand four enigmatic stones, remains of a circle of nine.

D There is a hermit's cave beneath Cratcliffe Rocks.

E The walk follows part of an ancient Portway.

F Viewpoint. Vagrants once mistook Robin Hood's Stride for a Manor House and visited it in the hope of receiving charity.

HARTINGTON AND ITS DALES
5 miles (8km) Easy/Moderate

Hartington has always been a busy village. Ancient Britons are believed to have fought Roman legionaries on nearby Hartington Moor. The village is mentioned in the Domesday Book as 'Hortedun' and had a market as long ago as the 13th century. Its church dates from the 14th century.

Many famous people have either lived or spent part of their lives around Hartington. Literary giants and philosophers, such as Dr Johnson, Byron and Mark Twain, came to admire the beauties of Dovedale. Jean Jacques Rousseau spent part of his exile close by. Without doubt, the most famous was Izaak Walton, author of the 17th-century treatise on fishing: 'The Compleat Angler — The Contemplative Man's Recreation'. Walton was a friend of Charles Cotton, his junior by 37 years, and the part of 'Compleat Angler' devoted to Dovedale tells of their adventures together. Cotton who lived at Beresford Hall, was a spendthrift, gambler and enjoyed the highlife, he was constantly on the run from his creditors.

Beresford Hall has long since disappeared and there have been no markets in Hartington for many years but the village is a hive of activity with the coming and goings of people from the surrounding farms and visitors who use it as a base to explore the Dove and its byways.

A Hartington Hall. A Jacobean house, at least 300 years old. Bonnie Prince Charlie is reputed to have slept here during the abortive march on London which got as far as Derby. The house was owned by the Bateman family, one of whom was knighted by Charles II. Another became Lord Mayor of London. Today Hartington Hall is a tastefully adapted youth hostel.

B Viewpoint. The limestone plateau extends in all directions. The prominent rise to the south west across Dovedale is Ecton Hill, one-time source of valuable copper deposits.

C Biggin Dale. Many uncommon plants and flowers grow on its rocky sides. The dale bottom, which only occasionally has surface water, supports blackthorn and other shrubby trees.

D Viewpoint. Rocky tors climb the valley sides above the Dove. This area is called Wolfscote Dale, Beresford Dale is nearer Hartington. Only that part downstream below Milldale is truly Dovedale but most people refer to the whole as Dovedale.

E The river is fordable at this point, an important packhorse crossing in olden times.

F Pike Pool. This deep pool was named by Cotton not, as it is said, because pike lived in it, but as a description of the slender spire or 'pike' of rock which reaches out from its depths.

G The Fishing Temple. This 'hideaway', shared by Walton and Charles Cotton, is, unfortunately, on private land and only its roof can be glimpsed through the trees. They sat here and contemplated their fishing exploits beneath a doorway marked 'Piscatoribus Sacrum 1674'. Their initials entwined in stone, mark their friendship down the centuries. Beresford Hall stood further back behind the wooded river bank. Leaving Dovedale, we can understand Walton's parting description of the River Dove as the finest river he ever saw and the most full of fish.

H Hartington is grouped around its duck pond in the market square. The village, has a couple of pubs and several cafés and shops. There is a dairy to the left of the pond where they make an excellent Stilton cheese, sold locally and in the factory shop just off the village centre. The Parish Church of St. Giles is well worth a visit for its mediaeval relics and attractive windows.

Over

0   1 mile

0   1 km

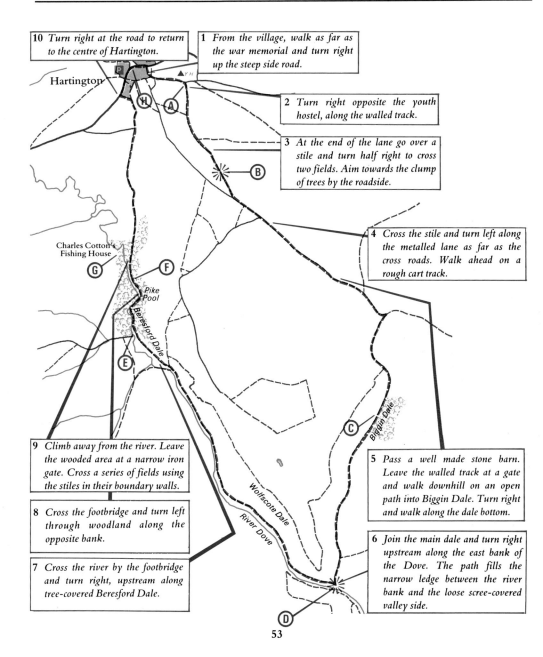

10 Turn right at the road to return to the centre of Hartington.

1 From the village, walk as far as the war memorial and turn right up the steep side road.

Hartington

2 Turn right opposite the youth hostel, along the walled track.

3 At the end of the lane go over a stile and turn half right to cross two fields. Aim towards the clump of trees by the roadside.

4 Cross the stile and turn left along the metalled lane as far as the cross roads. Walk ahead on a rough cart track.

Charles Cotton's Fishing House

Pike Pool

Beresford Dale

Biggin Dale

Wolfscote Dale

River Dove

9 Climb away from the river. Leave the wooded area at a narrow iron gate. Cross a series of fields using the stiles in their boundary walls.

8 Cross the footbridge and turn left through woodland along the opposite bank.

7 Cross the river by the footbridge and turn right, upstream along tree-covered Beresford Dale.

5 Pass a well made stone barn. Leave the walled track at a gate and walk downhill on an open path into Biggin Dale. Turn right and walk along the dale bottom.

6 Join the main dale and turn right upstream along the east bank of the Dove. The path fills the narrow ledge between the river bank and the loose scree-covered valley side.

53

Walk 33
HIGH TOR AND THE HEIGHTS OF ABRAHAM
4½ miles (7.2km) Easy

Matlock developed as a spa town during the Victorian era with an enthusiasm which culminated in the construction of the massive Smedley Hydro dominating the northern hillside above the town. The building is now used as the offices of Derbyshire Council. Thermal water still flows but, apart from its use in the indoor swimming pool of the New Bath Hotel, it is largely ignored.

The Victorians fancifully com- pared the local landscape to Switzerland and this walk cer- tainly has an alpine flavour. There is a cable car system from the foot of High Tor to the summit of the Heights of Abra- ham. The latter is an attractive area of landscaped woodland high above the Derwent Valley.

Small fees are payable to enter High Tor with its roofless caverns and woodland walks. A fee is also charged for entry to the Heights of Abraham. This covers show caves, other amenities and the cable car. A discount is normally available when embarking on the cable car by showing your copy of this guide.

From the Heights of Abraham, the walk follows a miners' path to Bonsall and its unique market cross. The route returns to Mat- lock by way of airy Masson Hill.

A Viewpoint. The River Der- went has carved a narrow gorge at the foot of the sheer limestone cliff of High Tor. On the oppo- site side of the valley, the wooded slopes of the Heights of Abraham lead to Masson Hill. Turn about and allow your eyes to follow the downward slope of High Tor. The hill which rises beyond is composed of gritstone lying on top of the limestone of High Tor. This is Riber Hill, dominated by a curious folly known as Riber Cas- tle. Built in the mid 1800s by John Smedley as a hydropathic hotel, it never flourished, mainly because there was a poor water supply and it fell into disuse in the 1940s.

Today it houses a zoo for rare breeds.

The summit of High Tor has a series of deep roofless caverns which can be explored without a torch.

B If following the alternative route, Matlock Bath's 'Swiss style' station is very much in keeping with the alpine flavour of this walk.

C The Heights of Abraham. This is a convenient refreshment stop. The name commemorates General Wolfe's battle with the French in 1759 to gain control of Canada. The Great Rutland Cavern is nearby. Here you can experience the sights and sounds of a working Derbyshire lead mine in the 17th century. The Victoria Tower is a few yards from the upper cable station and was built as part of a 19th-century 'job creation scheme'. The tower is a good vantage point for view- ing the surrounding scenery.

D The pillar of the market cross is mounted on a steep conical plinth which has 10 steps on its uphill side and 13 downhill.

E View of Bonsall village tucked in its hillside cleft.

Over

15 Go through a kissing gate at the bottom of the steep field. Climb down the flight of steps at the side of the large house and join the road into Matlock.

13 Keeping to the right of a boundary hedge, walk downhill through two fields towards the left hand side of Masson Lees Farm.

12 Cross the gravel lane and pass through the stile on its opposite side. Keep half right down the grassy hillside on a faint path. Cross ruined walls by stone stiles to be sure of the correct route.

11 Go through another squeezer stile into a narrow field.

10 Go through a stone squeezer stile in the right hand wall at the top corner of the field. Cross a small field keeping between two barns.

9 Turn right at a 'T' junction. Go through a field gate to follow first a hedge and then a wall on the right.

8 Follow the walled lane up a steep hill, to the right of the cross. Keep left at the end of the surfaced section to walk along a tree shaded path.

7 Turn right at the church and follow the road as far as the market cross. The 17th century Kings Head pub is opposite.

1 From Matlock, follow the riverside path through Hall Leys Park. Go under the railway

14 Cross the lane and enter the lower field through an old iron gate. Follow the hedge and cross field boundaries by their stone stiles.

Masson Lees Farm

Masson Hill

Masson Hill

Heights of Abraham

Matlock Bath

Bonsall

5 Follow the gravel track for about 40 yds (37m) beyond the upper cable car station and turn left along a level woodland path.

6 At a complex track junction by Ember Farm, bear right towards the farm, then left away from it, along the walled access lane and walk down to Bonsall village.

bridge as far as a footbridge. Do not cross, but turn left up a narrow lane.

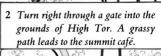

Matlock Bridge

Riber Castle (Fauna Reserve)

High Tor

2 Turn right through a gate into the grounds of High Tor. A grassy path leads to the summit café.

3 There are at least three alternative paths from High Tor, including one which follows a narrow ledge across the upper face.

4 Take the cable car to the Heights of Abraham. **Alternative to cable car:** follow the station approach and cross the A6. Climb Upperwood Road opposite as far as the lower entrance to the woodlands.

CROMFORD AND THE HIGH PEAK INCLINE
4½ miles (7.2km) Easy; one 530ft (162m) climb

Richard Arkwright came to Cromford in 1771 and built a cotton mill using the Derwent to power his newly invented spinning frames, completely revolutionising the textile industry. Part of his original mill is now a museum. Beyond it is the tow path of a preserved canal — the one time commercial lifeline of Cromford. The tow-path leads to the foot of Sheep Pasture, better known as the High Peak Incline.

The stark outcrop of Black Rocks marks the end of the climb and a track which was old long before Arkwright came to Cromford.

A The canal, built in 1793, gave Arkwright's mills a link with the developing Midlands. Today the canal is navigable, by horse drawn barge, as far as the High Peak Junction. In summer, it is therefore possible to use this novel mode of transport for the first 1¼ miles (2km)!

B High Peak Junction. The junction is between railway and canal.

C Sheep Pasture Incline. A plaque on the wall of the repair shop at the foot of the incline briefly explains the history of the 33 mile (53m) High Peak Railway. The line was opened in 1831 and was introduced as a means of connecting two canals — the Cromford and the High Peak, near Whaley Bridge. It was impossible to build a canal across the waterless limestone uplands but the railway was designed as though it was a canal. Rather than go round or through hills, the line climbs in a series of steep inclines, with motive power supplied by sta-tionary winding engines on the steepest. The line climbed to Parsley Hay and went on to Hindlow, above Buxton, before dropping into the Goyt Valley and Whaley Bridge by a further three inclines. As an indication of the canal mentality, stations along the High Peak were always known as 'wharfs'.

D Sheep Pasture Winding House. The tall building on the left of the track housed a steam powered winding engine to haul wagons up the incline.

E Viewpoint looking north along the Derwent Gorge. Cromford is below and you can see Willersley Castle in its parkland. The A6 cuts through the rocks of much widened Scarthin Nick. Looking upstream, Matlock Bath surmounted by the wooded Heights of Abraham and the bare limestone face of High Tor opposite, carry the eye towards Matlock Moor.

F Viewpoint. Dene Quarry is opposite. Massive steps or 'ben-ches' are cutting deep into the limestone hillside and gradually eating away Cromford Hill.

G Black Rocks. There was once an extensive lead mine beneath this point which is now marked by the overgrown spoil heaps and ruined buildings surrounding the Information Centre. A forest trail over the top of Black Rocks starts at this point.

H The lane is called Bedehouse Lane, an ancient way between Wirksworth and Cromford.

I North Street. The third storeys of the well-preserved cottages once accommodated handloom weavers' lofts.

J Cromford Mill. Richard Arkwright established the first successful water powered cotton mill on this site in 1771. The Arkwright Society has established a museum inside part of Cromford Mill which is dedicated to the father of the factory system.

Over

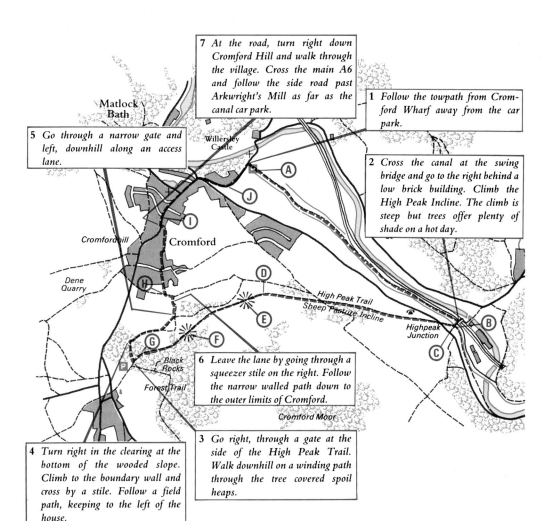

7 *At the road, turn right down Cromford Hill and walk through the village. Cross the main A6 and follow the side road past Arkwright's Mill as far as the canal car park.*

1 *Follow the towpath from Cromford Wharf away from the car park.*

5 *Go through a narrow gate and left, downhill along an access lane.*

2 *Cross the canal at the swing bridge and go to the right behind a low brick building. Climb the High Peak Incline. The climb is steep but trees offer plenty of shade on a hot day.*

6 *Leave the lane by going through a squeezer stile on the right. Follow the narrow walled path down to the outer limits of Cromford.*

3 *Go right, through a gate at the side of the High Peak Trail. Walk downhill on a winding path through the tree covered spoil heaps.*

4 *Turn right in the clearing at the bottom of the wooded slope. Climb to the boundary wall and cross by a stile. Follow a field path, keeping to the left of the house.*

CARSINGTON PASTURE
6¾ miles (10.9km) Easy/Moderate; two climbs of 333ft (101m) and 200ft (61m)

0			1 mile
0		1 km	

The small villages of Carsington and Brassington once depended on lead mining for their revenue. The stone cottages housed men who scratched a living below ground to supplement their income from part-time farming. Their small holdings are now incorporated within larger farms and the only tangible remains of mining are humps and hollows dotted along the walk.

10 Turn right through a stile and walk round the grassy hillside.

6 Leave the road by a gate on the left. Keep to the left of the prominent barn and cross a series of fields by lining up stiles in field boundary walls.

5 Turn right away from the trail at Longcliffe Wharf, then left along the road. (Stations were known as wharfs on the High Peak Railway.)

4 Cross the road by a couple of stiles and then turn left along the cinder track of the High Peak Trail.

3 Ignoring a stile, turn left to follow the line of the wall across Carsington Pasture.

7 Cross the head of an access lane and then walk across a rock strewn field to reach Brassington.

8 Enter the village by crossing a narrow lane and follow a narrow walled path on the right. Turn left through the village and then go past the Gate Inn and the Miners Arms to the second road junction

2 Climb a short flight of steps to reach the field on the right of the last house. There is no obvious footpath but climb the steep field by a zigzag route, aiming for the top right hand corner.

9 Cross the road, and keep right through the farmyard opposite. Go through a stile and turn right. Cross three narrow fields, and through stiles in their boundaries. Go left at the last one and climb to the top of the field.

11 Cross the lane and climb a couple of fields, aiming to the left of a group of tree shrouded rocks. Go over the brow of the hill.

12 Follow an improving track down to Carsington.

1 Start at the west end of Carsington's village street. Where the road turns sharp left, turn right along a short lane between groups of cottages.

(Map labels: Longcliffe, Longcliffe Wharf, Harboro Rocks, Black Rocks, Rainster Rocks, High Peak Trail, Carsington Pasture, King's Chair, Carsington, Brassington, B, C, A, D)

A King's Chair is a rough hewn seat carved from a limestone block on the opposite side of the wall. Do not cross as the field is private. The 'chair' looks out over the Henmore Valley and the new Carsington Reservoir.

B The High Peak Trail follows the track of the Cromford and High Peak Railway (see Walk 34).

C Harboro' Rocks and similar outcrops are made from dolomitic or magnesian limestone.

D View of Brassington. 'Branzicton' in the Domesday Book.

TISSINGTON AND PARWICH
3¾ miles (6km) Easy

0   1 mile

0   1 km

The two villages visited on this walk, on either side of the Bletch Brook, are built on ancient foundations. The houses of Tissington are grouped around the ancestral home of the Fitzherberts. Villagers decorate Tissington's five wells with floral pictures every Ascension Day as an ancient tribute to their pure water. Parwich is equally attractive in its own way but not as well known and, for some people, this could be an attraction in itself.

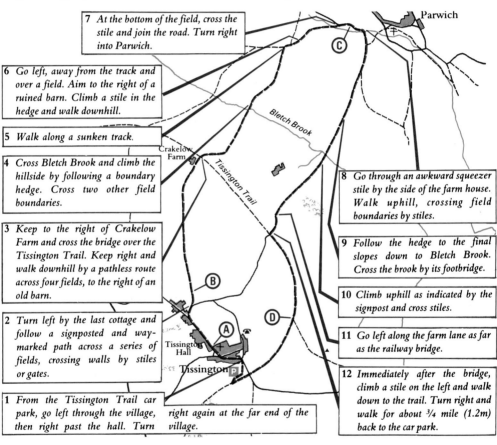

7 At the bottom of the field, cross the stile and join the road. Turn right into Parwich.

6 Go left, away from the track and over a field. Aim to the right of a ruined barn. Climb a stile in the hedge and walk downhill.

5 Walk along a sunken track.

4 Cross Bletch Brook and climb the hillside by following a boundary hedge. Cross two other field boundaries.

3 Keep to the right of Crakelow Farm and cross the bridge over the Tissington Trail. Keep right and walk downhill by a pathless route across four fields, to the right of an old barn.

2 Turn left by the last cottage and follow a signposted and way-marked path across a series of fields, crossing walls by stiles or gates.

1 From the Tissington Trail car park, go left through the village, then right past the hall. Turn right again at the far end of the village.

8 Go through an awkward squeezer stile by the side of the farm house. Walk uphill, crossing field boundaries by stiles.

9 Follow the hedge to the final slopes down to Bletch Brook. Cross the brook by its footbridge.

10 Climb uphill as indicated by the signpost and cross stiles.

11 Go left along the farm lane as far as the railway bridge.

12 Immediately after the bridge, climb a stile on the left and walk down to the trail. Turn right and walk for about ¾ mile (1.2m) back to the car park.

A Tissington. The hall was built in the early 17th century and the church is even older. When they dress the village wells, it is said they are remembering that the Black Death never reached here.

B Low ridges are the remains of mediaeval field systems.

C Parwich village has a delightful church. There is also a pub with a children's room.

D Tissington Trail. The trail, which was one of the first in the country to use old railway tracks, follows the Ashbourne–Buxton line to its junction with the High Peak trail near Parsley Hey.

Walk 37
ILAM HALL
4½ miles (7.2km) Easy

Tucked away on a bend of the Manifold river, Ilam village was built in the 1830s on the instructions of Jesse Watts Russell. The original Victorian houses of the village echo the fairytale image of the hall, built at a time when skilful labour was cheap. It was also a time when people could be moved at the whim of their landlords if, as in this case, he wanted more space or privacy.

The Ilam Hall we see today, with its Tudor style chimneys and mock Gothic architecture, is only part of the original building. The central tower and most of the formal rooms were demolished in the early 1930s. The rest of the building was about to suffer the same fate when it was bought by Sir Robert McDougall, a Manchester businessman. He had the remaining parts of the hall made habitable and presented it, together with the grounds, to the National Trust. Ilam Hall is now a youth hostel.

The hall and village replaced dwellings of a much earlier vintage. Their history can be traced back to Saxon times. St. Bertram hid himself in a cell near where the river bubbles to the surface below the hall. By his pious example, he persuaded the locals to abandon their pagan beliefs. He probably preached at the foot of the rough cross which now stands by his church. The carving on the cross is of Viking origin from around AD 900 – 1000. The church was 'improved' by Watts Russell and its 17th-century lines are broken by an octagonal mausoleum. The latter has a rather morbid but finely sculpted memorial to David Pike-Watts who is represented on his deathbed, surrounded by his daughter and her children.

The shaft of a stone cross was found in the foundations of a cottage during the rebuilding of the village. It now stands to one side of the riverside walk and is thought to date from around 1050, commemorating a battle between local Saxons and invading Danes.

Start the walk by following the riverside terrace where 17th-century dramatist Congreve wrote part of his comedy, 'The Old Bachelor', then climb above Hinkley Woods, known locally as Ilam Woods. Beyond, the walk joins the abandoned turnpike road from Cheadle (Staffs) to South Yorkshire via Thorpe. From Blore to Coldwall Bridge, the line of the turnpike can barely be traced through the lower fields and, as a result, the imposing bridge, which is now only used by local farmers and walkers, comes as a surprise.

A St. Bertram lived as a hermit in the small cave above the point where water bubbles out beneath a rocky overhang at the side of the path. The water has travelled for about 5 miles (8km) underground from Darfur Bridge near Wetton (see Walk 40) emerging at this point, as well as the stream bed near the footbridge at which you will shortly arrive.

In spring, the woods are full of anemones and celandines, then later primroses and bluebells compete for the sunlight as the trees come into leaf. Nature later creates its masterwork of subtle browns, reds and yellows as the beech leaves die every autumn.

B Battle Cross. Found when Watts-Russell rebuilt the village.

C Viewpoint. Ilam Hall can be glimpsed through the trees and beyond it rise Bunster Hill and Thorpe Cloud at the southern entrance to Dovedale.

D The 16th-century farmhouse, which is set back from the road, was formerly Blore Hall.

E Coldwall Bridge. Sturdy buttresses show how this bridge over the Dove has outlasted its need.

F Ilam village. The elaborate Gothic cross is a memorial to Mrs Watts-Russell, a constant reminder to the villagers of this not over popular lady.

Over

0   1 mile

0   1 km

2 Turn left over the second footbridge. Ignore the main path on the right beyond the bridge but follow a pathless course uphill towards the wooded skyline. Use a stone stile in a ruined wall as a route marker.

1 The walk begins from the car park in the grounds of Ilam Hall and follows the terraced riverside path.

9 Turn left past Dovedale House along the church path to return to Ilam Hall and its car park. There is a National Trust shop and café in the grounds.

3 Turn left on a grassy track. It is indistinct in places but, if in doubt, follow the boundary wall.

8 Climb the short flight of steps to the bridge and turn right, along the road into Ilam village.

4 Cross the dry valley and aim for the broad track which curves uphill around wooded Hazelton Clump.

5 Climb an awkward stile and turn left along the metalled road. Follow it over Blore cross roads to Coldwall Farm.

6 Turn left away from the road, go through the farmyard and into the field. Walk downhill, tracing the line of the abandoned turnpike road.

7 Keeping to the west bank (Blore side) of the river, turn left away from the bridge and walk upstream. Follow a fence above the hawthorn-covered slopes until a gap gives access to the riverbank.

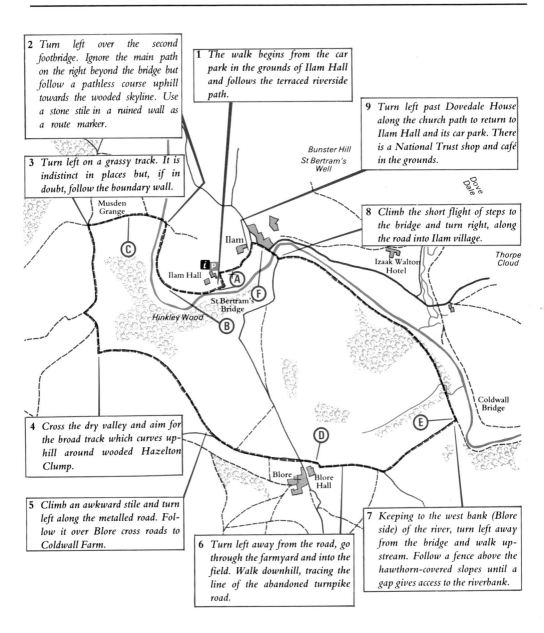

Bunster Hill
St Bertram's Well

Dove Dale

Musden Grange

Ilam

Thorpe Cloud

Izaak Walton Hotel

Ilam Hall

St Bertram's Bridge

Hinkley Wood

Blore
Blore Hall

Coldwall Bridge

Walk 38
THREE SHIRES HEAD
4 miles (6.4km) Easy

0 _____ 1 mile
0 _____ 1 km

Flash is the highest village in England, a place where winter starts early and lingers long after spring has arrived in more shel-tered places. The wind is keen but refreshing and the views are far ranging.

Counterfeiters once carried out their illicit trade in remote farmhouses around Flash and its name has since become linked with any suspicious or 'flashy' object.

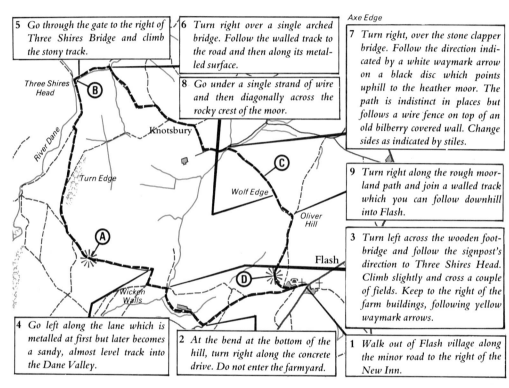

5 Go through the gate to the right of Three Shires Bridge and climb the stony track.

6 Turn right over a single arched bridge. Follow the walled track to the road and then along its metalled surface.

Axe Edge

7 Turn right, over the stone clapper bridge. Follow the direction indicated by a white waymark arrow on a black disc which points uphill to the heather moor. The path is indistinct in places but follows a wire fence on top of an old bilberry covered wall. Change sides as indicated by stiles.

8 Go under a single strand of wire and then diagonally across the rocky crest of the moor.

Three Shires Head **Ⓑ**

Knotsbury

Ⓒ

Turn Edge

Wolf Edge

Oliver Hill

9 Turn right along the rough moorland path and join a walled track which you can follow downhill into Flash.

Ⓐ

Flash

3 Turn left across the wooden footbridge and follow the signpost's direction to Three Shires Head. Climb slightly and cross a couple of fields. Keep to the right of the farm buildings, following yellow waymark arrows.

Wicken Walls

Ⓓ

4 Go left along the lane which is metalled at first but later becomes a sandy, almost level track into the Dane Valley.

2 At the bend at the bottom of the hill, turn right along the concrete drive. Do not enter the farmyard.

1 Walk out of Flash village along the minor road to the right of the New Inn.

River Dane

A Viewpoint looking south towards the dramatic outlines of Ramshaw Rocks. The uppermost boulders of the Roaches can also be seen, above the heather moors.

B Three Shires Head. The bridge which marks the junction of the counties of Cheshire, Staffordshire and Derbyshire once carried trains of packhorses and travellers on their journeys between Cheshire, The Potteries and South Yorkshire. Panniers' Pool, beneath the bridge, probably got its name as the resting and watering place for the pack animals.

C Viewpoint. Shutlingsloe, the crux of Walk 22, peeps invitingly over the moorland ridge opposite. Tiny moorland steads dot the valley sides. The land is so poor that the farms are no longer able to support full time agriculture and most are now run as part-time farms or even as second homes.

D Viewpoint looking down the Dane Valley.

VIATOR'S BRIDGE, MILLDALE
2¼ miles (3.6km) Easy

0   ½ mile
0   1 km

It is over 300 years since Izaak Walton fished in the River Dove with his impecunious friend, Charles Cotton of Beresford Hall. Apart from some modern traffic on the short stretch of road through Milldale, Dovedale and its famous trout stream have changed little since Walton and Cotton spent time on its banks, angling and philosophising. Walton referred to the Dove as being 'The finest river that I ever saw and the fullest of fish'. A sentiment true even today.

The route of the walk follows the river downstream from Viator's Bridge as far as the curious rock formation known as Dove Holes. A secluded dry dale on the left leads to Hanson Grange Farm before joining an ancient packhorse way back to Milldale.

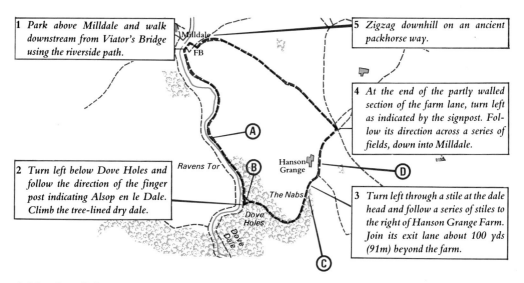

1 Park above Milldale and walk downstream from Viator's Bridge using the riverside path.

2 Turn left below Dove Holes and follow the direction of the finger post indicating Alsop en le Dale. Climb the tree-lined dry dale.

5 Zigzag downhill on an ancient packhorse way.

4 At the end of the partly walled section of the farm lane, turn left as indicated by the signpost. Follow its direction across a series of fields, down into Milldale.

3 Turn left through a stile at the dale head and follow a series of stiles to the right of Hanson Grange Farm. Join its exit lane about 100 yds (91m) beyond the farm.

A The thin alkaline soil on the craggy valley sides, supports many semi-alpine plants such as thyme and dwarf cranesbill. Rock outcrops on the opposite bank are used by local rock climbers.

B Dove Holes. These massive water-worn holes appear, at first glance, to be the start of an extensive cave system but are, in fact, only 20 feet/6 metres deep. This is a good vantage point from which to view the dale.

C The Nabs. These are the rocky crags guarding the exit from this dry dale.

D Hanson Grange. There were several extensive monastic sheep walks in the area until the Dissolution. Hanson Grange was part of one. The farm house looks Jacobean but is probably built on older foundations.

E Milldale. The Dove is crossed by the narrow packhorse bridge known as Viator's Bridge. The bridge earned its name from a reference in Izaak Walton's famous treatise, 'The Compleat Angler'. He referred to himself as Viator (The Traveller) and Cotton as Piscator (The Angler). To the left of the bridge stands part of Ochre Mill. It was powered by water which ran along the leat on the west side of the river below Shining Tor. Upstream was Lode Mill and the two mills gave Milldale its name.

Walk 40
THOR'S CAVE

0 ━━━━━━━━━━━━━━━━━━━━ 1 mile
0 ━━━━━━━━━━━━━━━━━━━━ 1 km

4 miles (6.4km) Moderate; one climb of 295ft (90m)

Starting at Wetton, an airy upland village, the walk crosses broad pastures before climbing down through an ancient coral reef into the Manifold Valley. A disused mill at this point is now a wel- coming café, well placed for a pause before the steep climb to mysterious Thor's Cave.

6 *Where the farm track turns right, go left following the boundary wall downhill. Move over to the right and then back by an awkward stile in order to avoid an area of dense scrub.*

5 *Turn right, along an access drive and left at its junction with another track.*

4 *Go over the stile in the corner of the field and climb the next to its top boundary. Climb the stile, cross a lane and go through a narrow belt of trees.*

3 *Bear right, away from the wall.*

2 *Go through stiles on either side of a small disused quarry. Follow a faint field path as far as the field boundary below Wetton Hill.*

1 *Park in Wetton and follow the village street past the church. Where the road turns left, follow the direction of the signpost to 'Back of Ecton'.*

7 *Continue down the dry valley, through the stockyard at Dale Farm and into the Manifold Valley.*

8 *Turn left along the valley road, then right and left over the river.*

9 *Go through a gate, away from the road, along the old railway track.*

10 *Turn left, over a footbridge and climb the hillside to Thor's Cave. Take care on the smooth slippery rocks.*

11 *From the front of the cave, follow the concessionary path and walled lane to Wetton.*

Sugarloaf

Wetton Hill

Wettonmill

Darfur Bridge

Wetton

Thor's Cave

A Viewpoint. Butterton church spire rises above the Manifold Valley.

B The prominent knoll to the left of the path is aptly called the Sugarloaf.

C Wetton Mill. Once ground flour for the surrounding villages.

D The valley section of this walk follows part of the route of the Manifold Valley Light Railway, a narrow gauge line which ran between Hulme End and Waterhouses from 1904 to 1934.

E Darfur Bridge. In dry weather, the River Manifold disappears underground at this point, reappearing near Ilam Hall.

F Thor's Cave makes a perfect frame for a breathtaking view of the Manifold Valley.

G Viewpoint. The slender spire of Grindon church stands out across the Manifold.